The Olden Time Series - Volume VI

HENRY MASON BROOKS

1886

TABLE OF CONTENTS

LITERARY CURIOSITIES

LITERARY CURIOSITIES

The following humorous lines well describe the difficulty that editors find in pleasing the public. They are expected to know everything, and to be able to satisfy all tastes and capacities. No imperfections can be excused in conductors of newspapers; they are not even allowed to be unfortunate.

THE EDITOR.

That editor who wills to please,
Must humbly crawl upon his knees,
And kiss the hand that beats him;
Or, if he dare attempt to walk,
Must toe the mark that others chalk,
And cringe to all that meet him.
Says one, Your subjects are too grave,
Too much morality you have,—
Too much about religion;
Give me some witch and wizard tales
Of slip-shod ghosts with fins and scales,
Of feathers like a pigeon.
I love to read, another cries,
Those monstrous, fashionable lies,—
In other words, those novels,
Composed of kings and queens and lords,
Of border wars, and gothic hordes
That used to live in hovels.

No, no, cries one, we've had enough
Of such confounded love-sick stuff,
To craze the fair creation;
Give us some recent foreign news
Of Russians, Turks, the Greeks, or Jews,
Or any other nation.
The man of dull scholastic lore
Would like to see a little more
In scraps of Greek or Latin;
The merchants rather have the price
Of southern indigo and rice,
Of India silks, or satin.
Another cries, I want more fun,
A witty anecdote or pun,
A rebus or a riddle;
Some long for missionary news,
And some, of worldly, carnal views,
Would rather hear a fiddle.
The critic, too, of classic skill,
Must dip in gall his gander quill,
And scrall against the paper:
Of all the literary fools
Bred in our colleges and schools,
He cuts the greatest caper.
Another cries, I want to see
A jumbled-up variety,
Variety in all things,—
A miscellaneous, hodge-pod print,
Composed (I only give the hint)
Of multifarious small things.
I want some marriage news, says miss:
It constitutes my highest bliss
To hear of weddings plenty;
For in a time of general rain
None suffer from a drought, 'tis plain,—
At least, not one in twenty.
I want to hear of deaths, says one,
Of people totally undone
By losses, fire, or fever:
Another answers full as wise,
I'd rather have a fall and rise
Of raccoon skins and beaver.
Some signify a secret wish

For now and then a favorite dish
Of politics to suit them.
But here we rest at perfect ease,
For should they swear the moon was cheese,
We never should dispute them.
Or grave or humorous, wild or tame,
Lofty or low, 'tis all the same,
Too haughty or too humble;
And every editorial wight
Has nought to do but what is right,
And let the grumblers grumble.
From a Salem paper of 1828; author not stated.
"All are needed by each one,
Nothing is fair and good alone."
Emerson.

In "old times" almost all the young ladies upon their marriage were "amiable" and "agreeable"; at least they are so represented in most of the announcements. The "maiden aunt" could not speak plainer in writing for the "Boston Sunday Gazette." We copy some specimens from Boston and Salem papers.

On Thursday last, in the Forenoon, was married Mr. Benjamin Davis of this Town, Merchant, to Mrs. Anstess Greenleaf, second Daughter of Stephen Greenleaf Esq; High Sheriff of the County of Suffolk.

The same Evening Mr. Oliver Wendell, of this Town, Merchant, was also Married to Mrs. Mary Jackson, only Daughter of the late Mr. Edward Jackson; both young Ladies of great Merit.
Sept. 13, 1762.

On Thursday Evening last Mr. Phillip Dumaresq, Merchant, was Married to Mrs. Rebecca Gardiner, third Daughter of Sylvester Gardiner, Esq; of this Town, an agreeable young Lady.
Dec. 19, 1763.

MARRIED]—Mr. Samuel Smith, to Mrs. Abigail Pittengill, an agreeable young widow.
Dec. 22, 1790.

Thursday evening last, John Whitney, Esq. merchant, of the state of Georgia, to the amiable Mrs. Bridget Seymore, of Wesport.
June 2, 1792.

—At Plainfield, Mr. Hezekiah Spalding, a batchelor of large fortune, aged 68, to the amiable Miss Mary Williams, aged 22!
1790.

MARRIED]—At Cambridge, Dr. J. Jennison, to the amiable Miss Belcher, daughter of his late Excellency Governour Belcher, of Nova Scotia, and grand daughter of his Excellency Jonathan Belcher, Esq. deceased, formerly

Governour of the then provinces of Massachusetts Bay and New-Hampshire.

Aug. 31, 1790.

—At Newbury-Port, Mr. WILLIAM YOUNG, of Boston, to the amiable Miss JUDITH WILLIAMS, of that town.

June 7, 1788.

NEWPORT, Nov. 24.

The 16th Instant, Mr. William Checkley, Son of the Rev. Mr. Samuel Checkley of Boston, was married to Miss Polly Cranston, a young Lady of genteel Acquirements, and of a most amiable Disposition.

Dec. 19, 1766.

BOSTON, January 12 [1767].

Last Thursday Evening Duncan Stewart, Esq; Collector of His Majesty's Customs for the Port of New-London, was married to Miss Nancy Erving, youngest Daughter of the Hon. John Erving, Esq; of this Town; a most amiable and agreeable young Lady.

Thursday last was married, at Newport, John Coffin Jones, Esq. of Boston, merchant, to the truly amiable and accomplished Miss Abigail Grant, daughter of the late Alexander Grant, Esq. a Lady of real merit, and highly qualified to render the connubial state desirable and supremely happy.

May 22, 1786.

—By the Rev. Dr. Stillman, Mr. Caleb Loring, distiller, to the agreeable Miss Polly Selsbry.

May 25, 1792.

MARRIED]—At Billerica, Mr. James Breed, to the amiable Miss Elizabeth Parker.—At Newtown, Mr. John Walter, A.B., to the agreeable Miss Polly Bullard.

March 24, 1792.

Married,

At Topsfield, by the Rev. Mr. Huntington, Mr. Joseph Averell, to the accomplished Miss Eunice Lamson.

Salem Register, 1801.

Editors were formerly very fond of curious matter for their lists of marriages and deaths. In the "Massachusetts Centinel" for 1789 the marriage of Pork and Hogg has a doubtful look, although it used to be supposed that everything in the paper was true.

MARRIED]—Lately in Delaware, Mr. ROBERT PORK, merchant, to Miss CATHARINE HOGG.—At Pepperell, Mr. GILES RICHARDS, of this town, to the amiable Miss SALLY ADAMS, youngest daughter of the late Rev. Mr. Adams, of Roxbury.—At Hull, Mr. SPENCER BINNEY, to Miss POLLY JONES, daughter of Mr. Thomas Jones, of that place.

A Boston paper of 1795 prints the following:—

MARRIAGES.

At Concord, Ebenezer Woodwrod, A.B., Citizen Bachelor, of Hanover, N.H., to the amiable Miss —— Robinson. At Longmeadow, Mr. John M. Dunham, Citizen Bachelor and Printer, as aforesaid, to the amiable Miss Emily Burt.

The promptness and decision which the said Citizens have shown——

"In all the fond intrigues of Love,"

is highly worthy of imitation; and the success that has so richly crowned their courage and enterprize, must be an invincible inducement to the fading phalanx of our remaining Bachelors, to make a vigorous attack on some fortress of female beauty, with a determined resolution,

——"Ne'er to quit the glorious strife,"

'Till, drest in all her charms, some blooming fair

Herself shall yield, the prize of conquering love!

In the "Salem Mercury," June 17, 1788, we find the following announcement, which reminds us of "Solomon Grundy, who died on Monday."

Died—At Rehoboth, Mr. Henry Bowen. He went to a wedding, well, on Thursday, taken sick on Friday, died on Saturday, buried on Sunday.

"Virtuous and amiable" were terms used frequently in the lists of deaths.

—At Portsmouth, Mrs. Jane Hill, the virtuous and amiable Consort of Mr. Elisha Hill. [1790]

The following is a list of marriages and deaths at various dates, taken from Boston and Salem papers:—

"Salem Gazette," July 19, 1811.

......MARRIAGES......

In Williamsborough (N.C.), Major Smith, of Prince Edwards (Va.), to Miss Charlotte B. Brodie.—This match, consummated only a few days since, was agreed upon thirty-one years ago at Camden (S.C.), when he was captured at the battle of Camden; and being separated by the war, andc., each had supposed the other dead, until a few months since, when they accidentally met, and neither plead any statute of limitation in bar of the old bargain.

"Salem Mercury," Oct. 21, 1788.

Married—In England, Mr. Matthew Rousby, aged 21, to Mrs. Ann Taylor, aged 89. The lady's grandson was at this equal union, and was 5 years older than his grandfather.

"Salem Gazette," 1817.

MARRIED,

In this town, Mr. Schuyler Lawrence, to Mrs. Chloe Minns, Mistress of the African School in Salem, and who has deserved well of the town and of the African race.

"Salem Register."

MONDAY, DECEMBER 3, 1827.

MARRIED

At New-York, by Rev. Mr. Hart, M.M. Noah, senior editor of the Enquirer, to Miss Rebecca, only daughter of Mr. Daniel Jackson, of that city. The junior editor of the Enquirer was on the same day killed in a duel. An old Bachelor at our elbow thinks the fate of the surviving editor most deserving of commiseration!

"Salem Gazette," 1811.

......DEATHS......

A short time ago, at the romantic village of Laughton-en-le-Morthen, in Yorkshire, England, Farmer Paul Parnell, late of the Ewes Farm House, age 76 years, who during his life, drank out of one silver pint cup with two handles, upwards of 2000l. sterling worth of nut-brown Yorkshire stingo (good old ale), being much attached to stingo tipple, of the best double stout, home-brewed quality. N.B. This calculation took at 2d. each cupfull.

"Essex Register," Feb. 5, 1824.

MARRIAGES.

In Solon, by Rev. Moses French, Josiah French, Esq., aged 48, to Miss Betsey Jackman, aged 40, being his fifth wife.

"Salem Gazette," Oct. 17, 1825.

At Rochester, N.Y., Capt. Samuel Currier to Miss Sally Clough—his sixth wife!

"Independent Chronicle," Nov. 23, 1797.

At Gloucester (R.I.), Mr. Elisha Herrenden, Æt. 83, to Mrs. Elenor Lushure, Æt. 88, being his eighth wife!

"Salem Gazette," 1829.

By Rev Mr Upham, Mr Lewis Plum, of Newark, N.J., to Miss Eliza P. Lemon, of this town.

"Essex Register," Dec., 1820.

At Beverly, on Wednesday evening last, by the Rev. Mr. Oliphant, Mr. Larkin Moore, travelling preacher, physician, poet, trader, andc., to Mrs. Nancy Cook.

"Salem Gazette," 1790.

Died]—At Horseley, in Derbyshire, England, a venerable matron, named Frances Burton, aged 107. She had practised midwifery upwards of 80 years. The husband of the above old lady was sexton of the parish church 70 years; and this ancient pair frequently boasted, that she had brought into the world, and he had buried, the parish twice over!

1807.

......DIED......

Near Gloucester, Virg., Elizabeth Wagner, aged 107. She never took medicine of any kind in her life.

From "Salem Gazette," 1811. Appropriate name for a rope-maker.

Mr. William Tarring, rope-maker, 38.

"Massachusetts Mercury," Dec. 27, 1799.

Died,

At Hamilton, Essex County, Plato Whipple, aged 103, one of God's images in ebony.

"Salem Gazette," 1811.

Mr. Jack Daland, a very worthy black man, aged 65. He was brought from Africa to the West Indies at about 11 years of age; but instead of being eaten, as he expected, by the white men, he was transferred by purchase to a happy asylum in this place, where he has spent upwards of 50 years of his life, respected by the whole town, as a faithful, industrious, pleasant-tempered, intelligent man. His honest industry was rewarded by the acquisition of a comfortable property, which he has left for the enjoyment of his family. The long train of white people who followed his remains to the grave, testify to the esteem in which he was held.

The following is a notice of a "distinguished merchant" and "literary" character of Newburyport, Mass. In the appendix to "Lord" Dexter's great production—where all the stops are placed together on the last page, so that "people can salt and pepper as they please"—we find these lines:

"All men inquire, but few can tell
How thou in Science doth excel!"

Timothy Dexter. The subject of the present sketch, according to his own account, was born in Malden, Massachusetts. "I was born," says he (in his celebrated work, "A Pickle for the knowing ones"), "1747, Jan. 22; on this day in the morning, a great snow storm in the signs of the seventh house; whilst Mars came forward Jupiter stood by to hold the candle. I was to be a great man."

Lord Dexter, after having served an apprenticeship to a Leather dresser, commenced business in Newburyport, where he married a widow who owned a house and a small piece of land, part of which, soon after the nuptials, were converted into a shop and tanyard.

By application to his business his property increased, and the purchase of a large tract of land near Penobscot, together with an interest which he bought in the Ohio Company's purchase, afforded him so much profit, as to induce him to buy up Publick Securities at forty cents on the pound, which securities soon after became worth twenty shillings on the pound.

His Lordship at one time shipped a large quantity of warming pans to the West Indies where they were sold at a great advance on prime cost, and used for molasses ladles. At another time, he purchased a large quantity of whalebone for ship's stays; the article rose in value upon his hands, and he sold it to great advantage.

Property now was no longer the object of his pursuit; but popularity became the god of his idolatry. He was charitable to the poor, gave large donations to religious societies, and rewarded those who wrote in his praise. His lordship about this time acquired his peculiar taste for style and splendour; and to enhance his own importance in the world, set up an elegant equipage, and at great cost adorned the front of his house with numerous figures of illustrious personages.

By his order, a tomb was dug under the summer house in his garden, during his life; which he mentions in 'A Pickle for the knowing ones,' in the following ludicrous style:—

"Heare will lie in box the first Lord in Americake the first Lord Dexter made by the voice of hampsher state my brave fellows Affirmed it they give me the titel and so Let it goue for as much as it will fetch it wonte give me Any breade but take from me the Contrary fourder I have a grand toume in my garding at one of the grasses and the tempel of Reason over the toume nand my coffen made and all Ready I emy house painted with white Lead an side and outside touched with green and bras trimmings Eight handels and a good Lock, I have had one mock fourrel it was so solmon and there was so much Criing about 3000 spectators I say my house is Euqal to any mansion house in twelve hundred miles and now for sale for seven hundred pounds weight of Dollars by me

TIMOTHY DEXTER."

Lord Dexter believed in transmigration sometimes; at others he was a deist. He died on the 22d day of Oct. 1806, in the 60th year of his age.

Salem Observer, Dec. 17, 1825.

From what we have heard and read of Mr. Dexter, it is a matter of surprise to us how such eccentricities could have attracted the attention they evidently did. It is doubtful if so much folly and conceit could now interest many people for any length of time.

Curious old almanacs.

An Old Almanack. A friend has handed us an almanack one hundred and fifty years old, which is quite a curiosity in its line. The following is the title:

"The New-England Almanack for the Year of our Lord MDCCIII. Being Third after Leap-year, and from the Creation, 5652. Discovery of America by Columbus, 211. Reign of our Gracious Queen Anne, (which began March 8, 1702,) the 2 year. Wherein is contained, Things necessary, and common in such a Composure. As the Quarters of the Moon, Aspects of the Planets and Weather set down Exactly according to the Aspects, Courts, Spring Tides, Rising and Setting of the Sun, Sun and Moons place, time of Full Sea at Boston, the Eclipses, High Ways, andc., with several other Curiosities. Calculated for the Meridian of Boston, the Metropolis of New-England, Lat. 42, 24, but may serve any part of the Country, (even as far as New-York,) without sensible Error. By Samuel Clough.

The Heavens to us, God's Glory do make known,

By th' Firmament, his handy work is shown.

Licensed by His Excellency the Governour. Boston: Printed by B. Green and J. Allen, for the Booksellers, and are to be Sold at their Shops. 1703."

Then follows a short address "To the Readers" of the Almanack. The figure of "Man's Body" with the "Twelve Signs of the Zodiack," is headed with the following lines:

The Anotomy must still be in,
Else th' Almanack's not worth a pin:
For Country-men regard the Sign
As though 'Twere Oracle Divine.
But do not mind that altogether,
Have some respect to Wind and Weather.

The months of the year are introduced as follows:

January.
Cold Weather now 'gins to be fierce,
And Norwest Winds our bodys pierce.
February.
The Weather still continues cold,
Therefore warm cloaths are good we hold.
March.
'T is the best Month of all the year,
Wherein to brew good napping Beer.
April.
Now Leaves on Trees begin to spring,
And Birds on Hedges sit and sing.
May.
To walk Five Miles in his own Farm,
Will do a Husbandman no harm.
June.
Now Countrymen each Sun shine day,
Mow down their Grass, and make it hay.
July.
If Mildew now blasts English Grain,
'Twill make poor Husbandmen complain.
August.
But if from Blasting it be free,
The Farmers then should thankful be.
September.
The Leaves from Trees now fall away,
And sweetest Flowers do decay.
October.
If Barns are full, though Fields be empty,
It doth prognosticate a plenty.
November.
One day this Month each Fruitful year,
Give thanks to GOD, and Eat good chear.

December.

The Weather now 'gins to be cold,

Which makes to shrink both young and old.

SATURDAY, DEC'R 24, 1853.

The Salem Observer.

Another Old Almanack. In our last we gave an account of an old Almanack for the year 1703. Since then we have seen another some sixteen years older, printed for the year 1687. It was bound in with an old account book that formerly belonged to the Rev. Thomas Barnard, a minister of Andover, from 1682 to 1718,—the great-grandfather of the Rev. Thomas Barnard, D.D., the first minister of the North Church in this city, who died Oct. 1, 1814, in the sixty-seventh year of his age, also an ancestor of Capt. Edward Barnard, of this city. We insert the title page and other extracts therefrom, which we trust will impart the same interest to our readers as we derived from its perusal.

It is prefaced by the following:

Novemb. 24th, 1686. I have Perused the Copy of an Almanack for the Ensuing Year, Composed by John Tulley, and find nothing in it contrary to His Majesties Laws, and therefore Allow it to be Printed, and Published by Benjamin Harris, Book-Seller in Boston.

Edward Randolph, Secr.

The following is the title:

Tully 1687. An Almanack for the Year of Our Lord MDCLXXXVII. Being the third after Leap-year, and from the Creation 5636. The Vulgar Notes of which are Prime 16—Epact 26—Circle of the ☉ 16—Domin: Letter B. Unto which is annexed a Weather Glass, whereby the Change of the Weather may be foreseen. Calculated for and fitted to the Meridian of Boston in New-England, where the North Pole is elevated 42 gr. 30 m. By John Tulley. Boston, Printed by S. Green for Benjamin Harris; and are to be Sold at his Shop, by the Town Pump near the Change. 1687.

Then follows "A Table of Kings," from William the Conqueror, 1066, to James 2d, 1685, closing with the lines—

Now may we look on Monarchy and sing,

In health and peace long live great JAMES our King.

And concluding with the "Weather Glass," andc., andc., which follow:

Prognostica Georgica: Or the Country-man's Weather-Glass.

Prognosticks of Tempests. The obscuring of the smaller stars is a certain sign of Tempests approaching, the oft changing of the Winds is always a forerunner of a storm.

Of Winds. The resounding of the Sea upon the shore, and murmuring of the Winds in the Woods without apparent Wind, shew wind to follow; shooting of stars (as they call it) is an usual sign of wind from that quarter the star came from, Redness of the Skie in the morning is a token of Winds, or Rain, or both: if the circles that appear about the Sun, be red and broken, they portend wind: if thick and dark, Winds, Snow, or Rain: The like may be said of the Circles about the Moon.

Of Rain. If two Rainbows appear, they are a sign of Rain: If the Sun or Moon look pale, look for Rain: if a dark Cloud be at Sun-rising, in which the Sun soon after is hid, it will dissolve it, and Rain will follow: if the Sun seem greater in the East than commonly, it is a sign of Rain, if in the West about Sun-setting there appear a black Cloud, you may expect Rain that night, or the day following, if in the winter time thick white Clouds appear in the South-east near the Horizon at Sun rising, they portend Snow, a day or two after: If black Clouds appear there, it is a sign of Rain.

Of Fair Weather. If the Moon look bright and fair, look for Fair Weather. Also the appearing of one Rainbow after a storm, is a known sign of Fair Weather. If Mists come down from the Hills, or descend from the heavens, and settle in the valleys, they promise fair hot weather: Mists in the Evening shew a fair, hot day on the morrow: The like when mists rise from the waters in the evening. Much more might be added, but I would not tire the reader.

It appears by the following that the first form of government, under the King, was accepted by the people in 1686.

May 14, 1686. Arrived from England, His Majesty's Commission to divers worthy Gentlemen, to be a President and Council for the management of his Majesty's Government here, and accordingly on the 25th of May, '86, the President and Council being assembled in Boston, the exemplification of the Judgment against the Charter of the Late Governour and Company of the Massachusetts-Bay in N E together with His Majesty's Commission of Government were publickly read, and received by persons of all conditions with general Acceptance.

It will appear by the following advertisement that a market was then first appointed by authority to be kept in Boston.

Advertisement. There is Appointed by Authority a Market to be kept in Boston, and a Committee is ordered to meet and state the place, and days, and other circumstances relating to the good settling thereof: Of which a more particular Account may be speedily expected.

This Almanack was published only 67 years from the settlement at Plymouth, and 59 from that of Salem.

In the eyes of the old New England people the almanac stood next to the Bible in importance. Almost the only knowledge we have of many events of those early days has been obtained from diaries kept in interleaved almanacs. It is true, important facts are often found recorded in connection with trifling or quite unimportant matters.

The venerable Dr. Holyoke, of Salem, president of the Massachusetts Medical Society, who died in March, 1829, at the age of one hundred years and eight months, wrote a letter, a few months before his death, in answer to a request that he would furnish some particulars of his mode of living. Dr. Holyoke was through life noted for being remarkably temperate in all things. After his death it was reported that some physician said (perhaps in fun) that if Dr. H. had not been in the habit of using intoxicating liquors he might have lived to a good old age.

We give here a copy of this interesting letter.

Salem.

SATURDAY MORNING, AUGUST 1, 1829.

Dr. Holyoke. The Medical Society of this District have rendered an appropriate tribute of respect for the memory of their venerated associate, the late Dr. E.A. Holyoke, by publishing an elegant little volume, containing a memoir of the deceased, prepared by a Committee of the Society, and a few of his writings. We have selected from the latter the following articles, which will interest the reader. The first is an account of Dr. Holyoke's habits of life, diet, andc., furnished by him in a letter to one of his friends; the others are a historical memorandum and a fragment of the Doctor's poetical effusions.

To —— —— —— Williamsville, Person County,

North Carolina.

Salem, Oct'r—1828.

Sir,—I received yours of the 20th ult. on ye 30th, wherein you wish me to give you some Account of my Mode of Life, andc.—In answer to which I would first mention that I was providentially blessed with an excellent Constitution—that I never injured this constitution by Intemperance of any kind—but invigorated it by constant Exercise, having from my 30th to my 80th Year walked on foot (in the Practice of my Profession)—probably as many as 5 or 6 miles every day, amounting to more than a million[A] of miles, and tho' sometimes much fatigued, the next Night's refreshing Sleep, always completely restored me. In early life, between 20 and 30, I used to ride on Horse back, but being often pestered by my Horses slipping their Bridles I found it more convenient to walk.

As to my Diet, having been taught to eat of any thing that was provided for me, and having always a good Appetite, I am never anxious about my food, and I do not recollect any thing, that is commonly eaten, that does not agree with my Stomach, except fresh roasted Pork, which tho' very agreeable to my Palate, almost always disagrees with me; for which however I have a remedy, in the Spirit of Sal Amoniac. Eight or Ten drops of Aqua Ammonia pura in a wine glass of Water, gives me relief after Pork, and indeed after anything else which offends my stomach. As to the Quantity, I am no great Eater, and I find my appetite sooner satisfied now than formerly;—there is one peculiarity in my Diet which as it may perhaps have contributed to Health I would mention; I am fond of Fruit, and have this

30 or more years daily indulged in eating freely of those of the Season, as Strawberries, Currants, Peaches, Plums, Apples, andc., which in summer and winter I eat just before Dinner, and seldom at any other time, and indeed very seldom eat any thing whatever between meals.—My Breakfast I vary continually. Coffee, Tea, Chocolate, with toasted bread and butter, Milk with Bread toasted in hot weather, but never any meat in my Life— seldom the same Breakfast more than 2 or 3 days running. Bread of Flour makes a large portion of my Food, perhaps near 1-2. After Dinner I most commonly drink one glass of Wine—plain boiled rice I am fond of—it makes nearly 1-2 of my Dinner perhaps as often as every other Day—I rarely eat Pickles or any high seasoned Food—Vegetable food of one kind or other makes commonly 2-3 or 3-4 of my nourishment—the condiments I use are chiefly Mustard, Horse radish and Onions. As to Drinks, I seldom take any but at meal times and with my Pipe—in younger Life my most common draft was Cider, seldom Wine, seldom or never Beer or Ale or distilled Spirits—But for the last 40 or 50 years, my most usual drink has been a Mixture, a little singular indeed, but as for me it is still palateable and agreeable, I still prefer it—The Mixture is this, viz. Good West India Rum 2 Spoonfuls, Good Cider whether new or old 3 Spoonfuls, of Water 9 or 10 Spoonfuls—of this Mixture (which I suppose to be about the strength of common Cider) I drink about 1-2 a Pint with my Dinner and about the same Quantity with my Pipe after Dinner and my Pipe in the Evening, never exceeding a Pint the whole Day; and I desire nothing else except one glass of Wine immediately after Dinner the whole day. I generally take one Pipe after Dinner and another in the Evening, and hold a small piece of pigtail Tobacco in my mouth from Breakfast till near Dinner, and again in the Afternoon till tea; this has been my practice for 80 years—I use no Snuff—I drink tea about sunset and eat with it a small slice of Bread toasted with Butter—I never eat any thing more till Breakfast.

I have not often had any complaint from indigestion, but when I have, abstinence from Breakfast or Dinner, or both, has usually removed it; indeed I have several times thrown off serious Complaints by Abstinence.—As to Clothing, it is what my Friends call thin; I never wear Flannel next my Skin tho' often advised to it, and am less liable to take cold, as it is called, than most people—a good warm double breasted Waist-Coat and a Cloth coat answers me for winter, and as the season grows warmer I gradually conform my Covering to it. As to the Passions, Sir, I need not tell you that when indulged, they injure the Health; that a calm, quiet self-possession, and a moderation in our Expectations and Pursuits, contribute much to our Health, as well as our happiness, and that Anxiety is injurious to both.

I had a good Set of Teeth, but they failed me gradually, without Pain, so that by 80 I lost them all.

Thus, Sir, you have, blundering and imperfect as it is, an answer to your Requests, with my best wishes that it may be of any service to the Purpose for which it was made—But must rely upon it that Nothing I have written be made public in my Name.[B] Wishing you long Life and many happy Days,

I am Yours, andc.

E.A. HOLYOKE.

P.S. I forgot to speak of my repose. When I began the practice of Physick, I was so often call'd up soon after retiring to Rest, that I found it most convenient to sit to a late Hour, and thus acquired a Habit of sitting up late, which necessarily occasioned my lying in bed to a late Hour in the Morning—till 7 o'cl'k in Summer and 8 in Winter. My Business was fatiguing and called for ample repose, and I have always taken care to have a full proportion of Sleep, which I suppose has contributed to my longevity.

Recollections and Memorandums of Past Events.

The first thing that I entirely remember was the funeral of Aunt Oulton, which was on July 18, 1732.

The first Aurora Borealis I ever saw, the Northern or rather Northeast Sky appeared suffused by a dark blood-red colored vapour, without any variety of different colored rays. I have never since seen the like. This was about the year 1734. Northern lights were then a novelty, and excited great wonder and terror among the vulgar.

In 1737, Square Toed Shoes were going out of fashion; I believe few or none were worn after 1737. Buckles instead of Shoe Strings began to be used about the same time, but were not universal in the country towns till 1740 or 1742. Very broad brim'd Hats were worn as early as I remember. My father had a beaver whose Brims were at least 7 inches; which when he left off, I remember I used to wear in the Garden, or in a shower, by way of Umbrella. They were all cock'd triangularly. And pulling them off by way of salutation was invariably the Fashion by all who had any Breeding.

Boots were never worn except on horseback, or snowy or rainy weather. They frequently had large broad Tops that reach'd full half way up the Thigh. But Boots did not come into general use till the close of the revolutionary war.

Funerals were extravagantly expensive. Gold Rings to each of the Bearers, the Minister, the Physician, andc., were frequently given when the family could but ill afford it. White gloves in abundance, burnt wine to the company, andc., andc. This extravagance occasioned the enacting sumptuary laws, which though they check'd did not entirely suppress the complaints till the commencement of the revolutionary war.

In 1749, it was reported the train band list of the town of Marblehead was equal to that of the town of Salem. The difference is now very great. I suppose Salem has at least twice the number of Marblehead.

[1749.][C] The Houses (in Salem) were generally very ordinary. The first handsome house was built by Mr. Jno. Turner, then Col. Pickman, then Mr. J. Cabot, andc.

There was but one ropewalk, and that was on the neck, inside the gate. But one tavern of any note, and that was an old house at the corner now occupied by Stearns' brick store. The Houses for public worship were only the old (first) church—the eastern parish—the secession from the first church—the Friends' meeting house, and the Episcopal church.

The number of Inhabitants was estimated at between 5 and 6000.

The Commerce of this town was chiefly with Spain and Portugal and the West Indies, especially with St. Eustatia. The Cod fishery was carried on with success and advantage. The Schooners were employed on the fishing banks in the summer, and in the autumn were laden with Fish, Rum, Molasses, and the produce of the country, and sent to Virginia and Maryland, and there spent the winter retailing their cargoes, and in return brought Corn and Wheat and Tobacco. This Virginia voyage was seldom very profitable, but as it served to keep the crews together, it was continued till more advantageous employment offered.

There were a few Chaises kept by gentlemen for their own use, but it was no easy matter to hire one to go a journey.

Salem Observer.

[A] This seems to have been a slip of the pen; the following is his own calculation, made in 1823, and which from his great degree of exaggeration falls short of half the actual amount. "If from my age of 20 to 80 years I have walked 5 miles a day, which is a moderate calculation, I must have gone in that 60 years,

109,500 miles.

And in the first 20 and last 15 years, 38,325

———

In 95 years probably, Total, 147,825

[B] This prohibition could only have regard to the period of his life time and was occasioned by that extreme modesty which always rendered it painful to the Doctor to be held up to the public notice.

[C] These remarks refer to the period of Dr. Holyoke's residence in Salem, preceding the revolution.

Dr. Holyoke during his whole life, it is said, was never fifty miles distant from the spot where he was born. He was the first person to receive the degree of M.D. from Harvard College; was the first president of the Massachusetts Medical Society; and he made in the course of his life three hundred and twenty-four thousand professional visits.

Antiquity of Nursery Rhymes.—Many of these productions have a very curious history, if it could only be traced. Some of them probably owe their origin to names distinguished in our literature; as Oliver Goldsmith, for

instance, is believed in his earlier days to have written such compositions. Dr. E.F. Rimbault gives us the following particulars as to some well-known favorites: "Sing a Song of Sixpence," is as old as the sixteenth century. "Three Blind Mice" is found in a music-book dated 1609. "The Frog and the Mouse" was licensed in 1580. "Three Children Sliding on the Ice" dates from 1633. "London Bridge is Broken Down" is of unfathomed antiquity. "Girls and Boys come out to play" is certainly old as the reign of Charles II.; as is also "Lucy Locket lost her Pocket," to the tune of which the American song of "Yankee Doodle" was written. "Pussy Cat, Pussy Cat, where have you been?" is of the age of Queen Bess. "Little Jack Horner" is older than the seventeenth century. "The Old Woman Tossed in a Blanket" is of the reign of James II., to which monarch it is supposed to allude.
Salem Gazette.
Some British opinions of Benedict Arnold.
"The good whigs of America," says a late paper, "may be assured, that the infamous Benedict Arnold's mansion is the very next to Tyburn,—a well chosen habitation for such an abandoned traitor: A step or two conveys him to that fatal spot, where the most guilty of all the miserable beings who have ever suffered, was perfectly innocent compared with him.—He lives despised by the nobility and gentry, and execrated by the people at large— countenanced by none excepting their Britannic and Satanic Majesties, and such of their adherents, respectively, who are looking for promotion under their royal masters."
By a gentleman from the southward we learn that it is expected Congress will fix their permanent residence at Philadelphia.
Salem Gazette, Feb. 26, 1784.
NEW-YORK, November 16.
By very recent accounts from St. John, Nova-Scotia, we are informed that Benedict Arnold, having attempted to JOCKY some of the inhabitants out of their property, but being detected, and the people being much exasperated, offered to deliver him up to the Americans for ten dollars; but alas! before the bargain was firmly agreed on, he made his escape to Halifax, and there got protection from the populace.
We are informed that Benedict Arnold lately sailed from New-Brunswick for London. It is said that his residence in America, even among the provincial Loyalists, was rather uncomfortable; he therefore wisely preferred being enveloped in the atmosphere of London to residing on a continent which had been the theatre of his traitorous acts, and consequently the occasion of more frequent reflections on the infamy of his crimes.
Massachusetts Gazette, November, 1786.
Receipt for apple-pudding, in 1788, with the apple and the pudding left out.
For the HERALD of FREEDOM.

How to make an APPLE PUDDING.
Being a curious, elaborate and sublime Dissertation,
never before published.
By YANKEE DOODLE, Esquire.
(In Continuation.)
Chapter.—How and about NAMES.
Nugæque canoræ.   Hor.

I LOOK upon it as the greatest happiness of my life, that fortune has given
me a name that corresponds with my nature and constitution. Patriotism is
the strongest passion; and I glory in being a Yankee.—A Yankee is any man
born in New-England—and New-England contains the three northern
States, and a certain little, pestiferous, pseudo Island. My countrymen
generally have the credit of being a good-natured, psalm-singing, religious
kind of men, very honest, but plaguy hard in their dealings—insomuch that
a Carolinian or a Georgian frequently swear that the very Satan himself
could never get to windward of them.

This puts me in mind of a story.—A certain Boston sea Captain, of a sloop
of 60 tons burthen, coming with a cargo of New-England rum, shoes,
cheese, potatoes, and other valuable commodities, into Broadway, which
you must know is a very narrow passage in the Appomatax, a branch of
James River in Virginia.—Before I proceed I must acquaint the serious
reader—and who is there but must be serious in reading the solemn truths I
am about to declare—that every iota of what I shall delineate in these
sacred depositories of facts, is TRUTH.——I am now about to elucidate
the psalm-singing, religious character of Yankees, by a TRUE STORY,
never before published.——When our Boston sea Captain, therefore, came
into Broadway, a Virginian comes a-board of him—and as he goes down
into the cabbin, had to stoop a little, because the cabbin was low—for, as I
said before, the sloop was 60 tons, although our religious sea-captain
entered but 40 tons at the Naval-Office: Howsomever he had a reserve of
conscience, for the Naval-Officer charged him for light money, when there
was not one light-house in all the ancient dominion.—But this is nothing to
my story.

N.B. I mean to give the good-natured reader a whole chapter on the art of
Story-telling.

Well, as I was saying, the Virginian being obliged to stoop—the stooping
caused his head to be bowed down; and looking down, he saw a book lying
upon the starboard locker.—Well, says he, and what the d——l—but I
think it expedient to omit the Virginian oath; for this man, not being a
moral man, swore consumedly, and did not know a bible by sight, but only
by hearsay.—And Captain, cried the Virginian, will you sell this bible of
yours: I hear it's a mighty clever book for children.—And why not for
grown people? cried the Captain, taking up the book. Why, quoth the

Virginian, because I mean my three boys, who are from 11 to 14 years old, shall be good scholards at their larning—they can all say their letters already, and the youngest can spell.—The Boston sea Captain opening the bible found these words: "Search the scriptures;" and without saying any thing himself, pointed out the passage to the Virginian.—Pugh! said the Virginian, and walked upon deck.—Now, to explain this mystery, you must know the Yankee sea Captain shewed him the passage to denote that he would sooner sell his soul to the d———l, than his bible to a Virginian;—and the Virginian said pugh! and walked upon deck, because he could not read.

Longevity. Since we published the examples of longevity, collected by the editor of the Medical Adviser, we have seen another list, which is supposed to comprise all, which can be found from the year 66 to 1799. The number of those who lived from one hundred and seventy to one hundred and eighty-five years is 3; from one hundred and sixty to one hundred and seventy, 2; from one hundred and fifty to one hundred and sixty, 3; from one hundred and forty to one hundred and fifty, 7; from one hundred and thirty to one hundred and forty, 26; from one hundred and twenty to one hundred and thirty, 84; from one hundred and ten to one hundred and twenty, 277; from one hundred to one hundred and ten, 1310. Total of those who survived a century, Seventeen hundred and twelve.———This writer could not have included in his list the examples of longevity which Russia furnished, for we frequently find in the bills of mortality of this country for a single year, twice the number of centenarians. We have before us the table of deaths for 1813, which gives the following remarkable ages. One 165;—three 135;—one 130;—fifteen 125;—thirty-three from 115 to 120;—fifty-three from 110 to 115;—one hundred and twenty-seven from 100 to 105;—fourteen hundred from 95 to 100;—two thousand eight hundred and forty-nine from 90 to 95;—four thousand four hundred and fifty-one from 85 to 90. Whole number of deaths 971,338.

Salem Observer, Oct. 29, 1825.

Boston shop-signs in 1789.

To read the signs in this town is a delicate, sentimental repast.—I hope Bostonians will never complain of want of amusement, while there is one sign standing. If I had time, I would certainly consult Milton, to see how he has arranged matters in his description of chaos.—I doubt not I could there get a hint for two whole chapters. I had as lief take a walk through Cornhill, as to go to the new-invented moral lectures.

Herald of Freedom.

A CURIOUS WOMAN.

We have often heard it said that men are curious, and we can well believe it; but now we find it recorded that there has been at least one curious woman. Read the following extract from the "Salem Gazette" of 1795:—

Married at Andover, Mr. Aaron Osgood to the curious Miss Ester

Wardwell.

"AWFULLY GOOD."

In our opinion the oft-repeated words "awfully good," "jolly fine," and similar expressions, which sound so "charmingly sweet" from the lips of interesting young ladies, are quite cast into the shade by language used in the following extract from the Portsmouth, N.H., "Oracle of the Day," Nov. 24, 1798:—

MARRIED]—In this town, on Sunday evening last, by the Rev. Dr. Haven, MARK SIMES, Esq. Deputy Post-Master, andc. to the elegantly pretty and amiably delicate Miss MARY-ANN BLUNT, youngest daughter of the late Capt. John Blunt, of Little-Harbour.

Genius of Hymen; Power of fondest Love!

In showers of bliss descend from worlds above,

On Beauty's rose, and Virtue's manlier form,

And shield, ah! shield them both, from time's tempestuous storm!

A few years since, a young gentleman at the University in Cambridge asked of a Collegian the loan of his Wirgil. The inelegant pronunciation of the word Virgil was burlesqued by the young Collegian in the following story, with which his invention readily supplied him:—Lately (says he) I set out on a woyage to Wersailles, with one Captain Winal, in a British wessel called the Wiper; but we soon met with a wiolent storm, which drove us into a port in Wirginia; where one Capt. Waughn, a wery wicious man, inwited us aboard his wessel, and gave us some weal and wenison, with some winegar, which made me wery sick; so I did womit like wengeance; (and added, reaching out the book) You may have my Wirgil, and welcome. This humor had the desired effect; the young gentleman saw the absurdity of doing such wiolence to the letter V, and has ever since spoke like other people.

Salem Gazette, April 26, 1791.

What Mr. Welby, an English gentleman, saw when he was in the United States in 1821. A very flattering picture of the West.

More Travellers' Stories.

From the National Gazette.

A new book of Travels in America has been recently issued in London which rivals the volumes of our old friends Weld, Ashe, Fearon, andc. It is entitled "A Visit to North America and the English Settlements in Illinois, with a winter residence in Philadelphia; solely to ascertain the actual prosperity of the Emigrating Agriculturist, Mechanic, and Commercial Speculator"—by Adlard Welby, Esquire, of South Rauceby, Lincolnshire. This esquire has said enough, should he be believed, to settle ultimately the point of the truth or falsehood of Godwin's notable doctrine, that we owe the increase of our numbers chiefly to emigration. No sane European would venture among us after having read Mr. Welby's book. He discovered that, in Philadelphia, living was very dear, comfort very uncommon, and good manners still more rare. Throughout his journey he found in the taverns "a system of impertinence, rudeness, rascality, and filth, rendered more intolerable by an antipathy to the English, in the brutal manifestation of which most of the Colonel, Doctor, and Squire, keepers of the taverns, were pleased to indulge." When he asked an hostler to call him early in the morning, he was answered that—he might call himself and be d——d. In the Western country he found no symptoms of hospitality— witnessed only idleness and licentiousness, and experienced every where brutal rudeness and unbounded extortion. The western people usually combine in cheating all travellers, and sometimes "rifle," that is shoot residents among them who do not choose to descend to their own level. In Illinois "a party proposed to each other coolly to go and shoot neighbour *****, who had behaved ill to them sundry times; it was agreed upon; they went to his field, found the old man at plough, and, with unerring aim, laid him dead." And Mr. Welby adds that the country would be desirable to live in, did not the folks shoot each other thus, and were they not half savages. The shooting case reminds us of a traveller's story which we heard at a dinner table abroad. A gentleman and esquire of strict veracity, like Mr. Welby, related, in order to shew how common was the calamity of the coup de soleil, or stroke of the sun, in the Island of Java, that sitting once in the house of an opulent merchant of Batavia, drinking a cool glass of Madeira after dinner, with the merchant's wife in the room, the lady was, in the twinkling of an eye, reduced to a heap of ashes by a coup de soleil; when the husband observed to his guest, "don't be alarmed—we are accustomed to this;" then rang the bell with great composure, and on the appearance of the servant, coolly said—"Boy—sweep your mistress out, and bring us clean glasses."

In the neighborhood of Mr. Birbeck's settlement in Illinois, Mr. Welby could obtain neither eggs, milk, sugar, salt, nor water; and when he and his party sent a request to Mr. Birbeck for some water, the answer returned was, he made it a general rule to refuse every one. Mr. Birbeck is represented as having deceived and disappointed most of the English who were lured to his settlement by his "Journal." Mr. W. could discover none of "the snug cottages, with adjoining piggeries, cowsteads, gardens and orchards," which Mr. B. had introduced into his canvass. He found nothing but the primitive log building, that served the whole family—"for parlour, for kitchen, and hall." "The strange heterogeneous mixture of characters," says Mr. W. "which are collected here by the magic pen of Morris Birbeck, is truly ludicrous. Among many others, a couple now attend to the store at Albion who lately lived in a dashing style in London, not far from Bond-street; the lady brought over her white satin shoes and gay dresses, rich carpets, and everything but what in such a place she would require—yet I have understood that they have accommodated themselves to their new situations, hand out the plums, sugar, whiskey, andc., with tolerable grace, and at least 'do not seem to mind it.'"

In one of the principal literary journals of London, Mr. Welby's book is recommended as "carrying on its front the stamp of plain dealing, truth and candor, and entitled, from internal evidence, to the highest authority amid the conflicting statements and opinions respecting emigration to America." The reviewer adds:—"From a country so destitute of moral beauty as the author depicts it, so disgusting in its human externals, and so low in the scale, not merely of refinement, but of good principles, we are happy to withdraw." As Mr. Welby spent a winter in Philadelphia, and had acquaintance here, it is probable that such of the latter as have not seen his book will be pleased to know the complexion of its contents.

Salem Register, May 18, 1822.

In the "Essex Register" of July 18, 1833, may be found the following notice of two well-known American authors:—

Discourse on Genius. The Richmond Compiler speaks in terms of great praise of a discourse delivered recently in Richmond, before a Young Men's Society, by Joseph Hulbert Nicholas. A number of extracts are also given in the Compiler, as specimens of the performance, from which we take the following notices of two of our fellow-townsmen.—Boston Courier.

Of Charles Sprague, of Massachusetts, no language can be spoken but that of unqualified praise. Forsaking the modern school of writing, he is contented with being simple and natural. Sublimity, tenderness, wit, elegance, and beneficial satire characterise his muse.—The only complaint I have ever heard made of him is that he does not write more.

Of Nathaniel Parker Willis, a native of Massachusetts, and a fellow-student with myself at Yale College, I come now to speak. Of him I shall speak familiarly, as of an intimate friend; and impartially and justly, as one who wishes him well. Willis, I venture to pronounce the most remarkable genius our country has yet produced. I do not call him remarkable merely for his unusual precocity of song, but remarkable for the possession of that rare genius, which by any man, young or old, in our land, I do not think has ever been displayed. Nature has done wonderful things for him; but alas! he has thus far done but little for himself. The great pieces he has sometimes given us have cost him but little effort, and he has thrown out his productions, in prose as well as poetry, with a profusion and a variety that seem miraculous; and yet, of all our bards, he has met with the most severe and merciless censures. In some measure he has deserved the treatment. In College he would not condescend to study, and charity only for his high genius enabled him to gain a degree. Besides, he gained his first and best reputation by pieces founded upon scriptural subjects, and he stood committed to the world as a religious man. Many who had never seen aught of him but his productions, and had formed the loftiest estimate of his personal character from the pure tendency of his effusions, were astonished and grieved when introduced to the author.—His head made giddy by the praises of young and old, he forgot himself, and possessing most shrewd good sense, he would talk the reverse. He became fantastic in apparel, as he did likewise in his style of writing; made himself too common, and almost broke a pious father's heart by deserting the altar of that divine Jesus upon whose Bible he had founded the fairest fabric of his fame. My friend, of whom I so sternly speak, is now in Italy; and should these remarks, per chance, ever meet his eye, I beseech him by our past friendship, by our walks "by moon or glittering star-light," through the Eden groves and avenues of New-Haven, by the love he bears to his parents, and above all, by the love he bears that Saviour, upon whose image and the scenes of whose mortal pilgrimage he is rapturously gazing, in the matchless pictures of the Italian masters, I beseech him, when he returns to his native land, to wear no longer a ridiculous mask, but to appear in his own native strength, dignity, and surpassing loveliness.

In the "Salem Observer," March 8, 1834, are to be found the following references to well-known young ladies of the day. Miss Silsbee is supposed to be the daughter of the Hon. Nathaniel Silsbee, of Salem, Massachusetts senator in Congress. She afterwards married Jared Sparks, the well-known historian, president of Harvard College, etc.

High Life at Washington. The Washington Correspondent of the Boston Morning Post, in describing Gov. Cass's soiree, thus notices some of the young ladies who were present:—

Miss Keyser of Baltimore, uniting youth and beauty, possesses an eye as dark as the absence of all light, beaming with a lustre that eclipses all. I never saw a countenance betoken such perfect happiness; it was like a star-lit lake, curling its lips into ripples in some dream of delight, as the west wind salutes them with its balmy breath and disturbs their placid slumber. I never before realised Byron's idea of

"Music breathing o'er the face;"

till Miss Keyser's brought it home to the business and bosom.

Miss Silsbee, of Salem, with a form of great symmetry, possesses a countenance not only beautiful, but entirely intellectual—the most so of any you have met with either here or elsewhere; it is of the Italian model; and should have basked beneath an Italian sky. She is very easy, graceful and modest in her deportment, and dresses 'rich not gaudy;' the cameo necklace that graced her person was only the foil that set off the diamond.

Miss Harper of Baltimore, with a fine face and form, is particularly unrivalled for a bust of unrivalled symmetry; it would furnish a model for a Canova; and reminds me of Greenough's Medora.

Miss M'Lane of this city, with many separate charms that could not fail of attraction, unites with them the finest of fine forms.

And last, not least, the younger Miss Cass possesses the most perfect Madonna countenance I have ever seen clothed in living lustre. It was one of the first that attracted my attention when I entered the saloon, and the last that received my parting glance when I retired; it seemed to be—
"While in, above the world;"
I am told it is entirely characteristic; that she is in heart and thought, what you behold in her countenance—happy, but not gay; serious but not sad; devout, yet not a devotee.

In the "Salem Gazette" of 1815 is the following curious information about Scott's novels, which shows how easy it is for people to be mistaken.

William Erskine, Esq. is said to be the author of the new and interesting Novel, "Guy Mannering."—Walter Scott had been pronounced the author.

Waverly.—It is not yet decided to whom this very interesting novel belongs. It came into the world with all the advantage that the name of Walter Scott could give it; but Guy Mannering's appearance seems to have dissolved that connection. An article in our first page attributes the work to Wm. Erskine; but in the last North-American Review we read the following:—"An English Magazine says, the author of Waverly and Guy Mannering is a young gentleman of the name of Forbes, the son of a Scotch baronet." The Review remarks, that the extract in the title page of the latter, from the Lay of the Last Minstrel, was a delicate way of informing the public that they were under a mistake in attributing the former to Walter Scott.

On the 16th June, 1806, there was a total eclipse of the sun. The following is all the "Salem Gazette" of the 17th has to say of such a remarkable event.

Yesterday the great Solar Eclipse took place, agreeably to the calculations which had been made. The day was very favourable to viewing it. The air was remarkably clear, and there was not a cloud in the hemisphere. As the sun shut in, the stars appeared, and many were visible at the time of total darkness. A considerable alteration in the temperature of the atmosphere was felt during the continuance of the Eclipse.

In the "Boston Palladium" of 1819, copied from a London paper, is Lord Mansfield's opinion about a word in Johnson's Dictionary. In the original editions of this work are to be found many very curious definitions, some of which bore so hard upon the government as to be construed into libel.

FROM A LONDON PAPER.

EXCISE.

The following curious little document is the opinion of Lord Mansfield, when Attorney-General, upon Dr. Johnson's explanation of the word Excise:—

CASE.

Mr. Samuel Johnson has lately published a book, entitled "A Dictionary of the English Language, in which the words are deduced from their originals, and illustrated in their different significations by examples from the best writers. To which are prefixed a History of the Language and an English Grammar."

Under the title "Excise" are the following words:—

Excise, n.s. (accijs, Dutch; excisum, Latin,) a hateful tax levied upon commodities, and adjudged not by the common judges of property, but wretches hired by those to whom "Excise" is paid.

The people should pay a rateable tax for their sheep, and an Excise for every thing which they should eat.—Hayward.

"Ambitious now to take excise Of a more fragrant paradise."—Cleveland.

EXCISE.

"With hundred rows of teeth the shark exceeds, And on all trades, like Cassawar, she feeds."

Marvel.

"Can hire large houses and oppress the poor By farm'd Excise."—Dryden's Juvenal, Sat. 3.

The Author's definition being observed by the Commissioners of Excise, they desire the favour of your opinion:

Qu.—Whether it will not be considered as a libel; and if so, whether it is not proper to proceed against the author, printers and publishers thereof, or any and which of them, by information or how otherwise?

OPINION.

"I am of opinion that it is a libel; but under all the circumstances, I should think it better to give him an opportunity of altering his definition; and in case he don't, threaten him with an information.

"(Signed)   W. MURRAY.

"29th Nov, 1755."

Samuel Sewall, whose remarkable "Diary" has within a few years been printed by the Massachusetts Historical Society, appears to have been the successor of John Foster, who printed the first book ever issued from the press in Boston,—namely, "Hubbard's Election Sermon,"—in 1676. All previous printing in the colony had been executed at Cambridge. Mr. Hubbard was the minister of Ipswich.

SAMUEL SEWALL.

When John Foster (the first who carried on printing in Boston) died in 1681, the town was without the benefit of the press; but a continuance of it being thought necessary, Samuel Sewall, not a printer but a magistrate, and a man much respected, was selected as a proper person to manage the concerns of it, and as such was recommended to the general court. In consequence of this recommendation, the court, in Oct. 1681, gave him liberty to carry on the business of printing in Boston. The license is thus recorded: "Samuel Sewall, at the instance of some Friends, with respect to the accommodation of the public, being prevailed with to undertake the Management of the Printing Press in Boston, late under the command of

Mr. John Foster, deceased, liberty is accordingly granted to him for the same by this court, and none may presume to set up any other Press without the like Liberty first granted."

Sewall became a bookseller.—Books for himself and others were printed at the press under his management; as were several acts and laws, with other works for government. Samuel Green, jun., was his printer. In 1682 an order passed the general court for the treasurer to pay Sewall ten pounds seventeen shillings, for printing the election sermon, delivered that year by the Rev. Mr. Torrey.

In 1684, Sewall, by some means, was unable to conduct the press, and requested permission of the general court to be released from his engagement. This was granted; the record of his release is in the words following.

"Samuel Sewall by the providence of God being unable to attend the press, andc., requested leave to be freed from his obligations concerning it, which was granted, with thanks for the liberty then granted."

In 1684, and for several subsequent years, the loss of the charter occasioned great confusion and disorder in the political concerns of the colony. Soon after Sewall resigned his office as conductor of the press in Boston, he went to England, and he returned in 1692. He was undoubtedly the same Samuel Sewall who, when a new charter was granted by king William, was for many years one of the council for the province, and who, in 1692, was appointed one of the Judges of the Superior Court; in 1715 Judge of Probate; and in 1718, Chief Justice of Massachusetts. He died Jan. 1, 1729, aged 78 years.— Boston News Letter.

Knowledge of natural history at the Isles of Shoals in the early part of the last century.

A Century Ago. The N. York Gazette relates that when Rev. Mr. Tuck, in the early part of the last century, was ordained minister of Star Island, one of a cluster called the Isles of Shoals, his parish offered him, beside the usual parsonage house, a quintal of fish each family, but no money, as a salary. It is well known that the fish cured at these islands are called dun fish, and have the highest reputation for excellence wherever known. They are caught in the depth of winter, and are fit for market before the hot weather. They derive the name of dun from the color which they assume. There were at the period of which we speak, about fifty families in the cluster, giving him fifty quintals per year. The average price of a dun fish is about ten dollars, and the worthy pastor always procured a ready sale for them, thereby realizing his five hundred dollars per annum. With this stipend he flourished, and brought up a family, whom he educated himself, and fitted one of his sons for entrance into Harvard College. The lad had never been away from the Shoals till he reached Long wharf on his way to Cambridge. He had never seen a horse, nor heard a church bell. On landing, he saw many horses attached to various vehicles; and speaking to his father, said, "Only see what queer cows they have in Boston! they are not shaped like ours, and are all without horns." In passing by the Old South, in Cornhill, the big bell of that church struck up a peal, the effect of which nearly drove the young man mad.

Salem Observer[1829].

What Captain Hall, R.N., thought of a Salem gentleman.

From Capt. Basil Hall's Travels in America—just published.

We reached the town of Salem in good time for dinner; and here I feel half tempted to break through my rule, in order to give some account of our dinner-party, chiefly, indeed, that I might have an opportunity of expatiating—which I could do with perfect truth and great pleasure—on the conversation of our excellent host. For I have rarely, in any country, met a man so devoid of prejudice, or so willing to take all matters on their favorable side, and withal, who was so well informed about every thing in his own and in other countries, or who was more ready to impart his knowledge to others.

To these agreeable attributes and conversational powers he adds such a mirthfulness of fancy, and genuine heartiness of good-humour, to all men, women, and children who have the good fortune to make his acquaintance, that I should have no scruple—if it were not too great a liberty—in naming him as the person I have been most pleased with in all my recent travels.

After dinner, we repaired to the Museum, the rich treasures of which have been collected exclusively by captains or supercargoes of vessels out of Salem, who had doubled one or other of the great southern promontories,—the Cape, and the Horn, as they are technically called by seamen. As my eye fell on numberless carefully cherished objects, which I had often seen in familiar use on the other side of the globe, my imagination revelled far and wide into regions I may never live to see again.

Salem Observer, 1826.

Compliment to New England. In a speech made by Mr. Lyell, the eminent geologist, at a late meeting of the British Geological Association, he said— "Were I ever so unfortunate as to quit my native land to reside permanently elsewhere, I should without hesitation choose the United States for my second country, especially New England, where a population of more than two millions enjoys a higher average standard of prosperity and intellectual advancement than any other population of equal amount on the globe."

Salem Observer, 1843.

Mrs. Trollope avers that pigs are caressed by the ladies and gentlemen of New York.

"REFUGEE IN AMERICA."

New-York and Boston. Mrs. Trollope, in her new work, called the Refugee in America, introduces some queer comparisons between the manners of

the two cities. We quote for example:—"In Boston, there are no persons allowed to vote at the elections of President or Governor of that province but native born yankees; while at New-York, emigrants are forced from the ships in which they arrive directly to the hustings, which are kept open the first two weeks of every month at Mason's lodge, Broadway, where they are allowed to jostle off the sidewalks the most respectable inhabitants. If they are reproved for such conduct, the answer invariably is,—'Isn't this a land of liberty?' I was one forenoon myself stopped at the lodge and offered a vote, with the preliminary question,—'Are you a Clay or a Jackson man?' In Boston, a person seen with a segar in his mouth in the street, is counted a blackguard; but in New-York no gentleman makes his promenade without one. In Boston, a housekeeper would be placed at the Sessions dock for suffering the refuse of his mansion to be thrown into the street; while in N. York he would be fined $1 if he allowed it to be thrown elsewhere near his premises. Swine is a Bostonian's bane, and a N. Yorker's antidote,—indeed this animal is as much caressed by the ladies and gentlemen of the latter city, as a lap-dog in London or Paris. The Governor and his twenty chosen ministers have made it a capital offence to molest one of these interesting quadrupeds while roaming the streets!"—[Oh! what a lying jade!]
Salem Observer, Oct. 13, 1832.

Early Accounts of New-England. The first settlers of New-England must have been blessed with singular powers of vision. One of them speaks of lions in Cape Ann: another (Josselyn), who arrived at Boston in 1663, and resided in this Colony about eight years, says of our frogs, "some, when they sit upon their breech, are a foot high, and some as long as a child one year old." He likewise says "old barley frequently degenerates into oats" in New-England.

"Enthusiasm" is described as a nervous disorder by Dr. Douglass, author of the Historical Summary.

Dr. Douglass's Notice of Salem. In looking over Dr. Douglass' historical summary, we found the following note on Salem. The author formerly lived in Boston, and after his removal to England, published his work in 1749. As he was a physician, he probably considered himself authorized to broach new theories. He certainly showed his ingenuity in imputing to our soil a tendency to produce the diseases of which he makes mention. It is perhaps fortunate for us that the Doctor did not live in our day, as he would have found in the excitement which has recently prevailed here in relation to the Mill Dam, Theatre, andc., new proofs of the correctness of his hypothesis.

"In Salem and its neighborhood Enthusiasm and other nervous disorders seem to be endemial. Hypochondriack, hysterick, and other maniack disorders prevail there, and Ipswich adjoining, to this day."
Salem Register, 1826.

Beer and cider "Federal liquors."

PHILADELPHIA, July 23 [1788].

A correspondent wishes that a monument could be erected in Union Green, with the following inscription:—

IN HONOUR OF

AMERICAN BEER and CYDER.

It is hereby recorded, for the information of strangers and posterity, that 17000 people assembled on this Green, on the 4th of July, 1788, to celebrate the establishment of the Constitution of the United States, and that they separated at an early hour, without intoxication or a single quarrel. They drank nothing but Beer and Cyder. Learn, reader, to prize those invaluable federal liquors, and to consider them as the companions of those virtues which can alone render our country free and respectable.

Learn likewise to despise

SPIRITUOUS LIQUORS, as antifederal;

and to consider them as the companions of all those vices which are calculated to dishonour and enslave our country.

In these "awfully fine" times, the following lines ought to be interesting:—

......POETRY......

From the Lady's Miscellany.

YANKEE PHRASES.

AS sound as a nut o'er the plain,
I of late whistled chuck full of glee,
A stranger to sorrow and pain,
As happy as happy could be.
As plump as a partridge I grew,
My heart being lighter than cork;
My slumbers were calmer than dew,
My body was fatter than pork.
Thus happy, I hop'd I should pass
Slick as grease down the current of time;
But pleasures are brittle as glass,
Although as a fiddle they're fine.
Jemima, the pride of the vale,
Like a top nimbly danc'd o'er the plains;
With envy the lasses were pale,
With wonder stood gazing the swains.
She smil'd like a basket of chips,
As tall as a may-pole her size—
As sweet as molasses her lips—
As bright as a button her eyes.
Admiring, I gaz'd on her charm,
My peace that would trouble so soon,
And thought not of danger nor harm,

Any more than the man in the moon.
But now to my sorrow I find
Her heart is as hard as a brick,
To my passion forever unkind,
Though of love I am full as a tick.
I sought her affection to win,
In hope of obtaining relief;
Till I like a hatchet grew thin,
And she, like a haddock, grew deaf.
I late was as fat as a doe,
And playful and spry as a cat;
But now I am as dull as a hoe,
And as lean and as weak as a rat.
Unless the unpitying fates
With passion as ardent will cram her,
As certain as death or as rates,
I soon shall be dead as a hammer.
Salem Gazette, April 5, 1811.
Gentlemen and children have sometimes been considered bugbears.
Boarders Wanted.
Two or Three Ladies can be accommodated with Board, on reasonable terms, in a small family, 18 miles from town, where there are neither Gentlemen or Children; a Stage passes the house twice a week, and the Middlesex Canal Boat near it every other day. Inquire at the Centinel Counting Room.
Columbian Centinel, July 25, 1812.
LIBERAL DONATIONS
Of the Legislature of New-York to the University of that State: 1,500l. for the Library; 200l. for chemical apparatus; 1,200l. for a wall round the College; 5,000l. for erecting a Hall, and additional wing to the College; 750l. for five years annually, for the salaries of additional Professors.—Blush! Citizens of Massachusetts, for your Legislators—who have so frequently denied relief to your University!!!
Columbian Centinel, May 5, 1792.
The books children read in 1789.
A great Variety of
Children's Books
Neatly printed, and adorned with elegant Cuts, are sold by T.C. CUSHING, at the Printing-Office in Salem—viz.
Little ROBIN RED-BREAST.
Memoirs of a PEGTOP.
The SUGAR-PLUMB; or, sweet Amusement for leisure hours.
The JUVENILE BIOGRAPHER, containing the Lives of little Masters and

Misses.

Be MERRY and WISE; or, the Cream of the Jests, and the Marrow of Maxims, for the Conduct of Life.

The HOLY BIBLE abridged.

History of little KING PIPPIN.

History of GILES GINGERBREAD.

History of TOM JONES.

History of Master JACKEY and Miss HARRIOT.

History of CHARLES CAREFUL and HARRY HEEDLESS.

Mother GOOSE's Melody.

The Exhibition of TOM THUMB.

Tom Thumb's SONG BOOK.

The FATHER's Gift.

The MOTHER's Gift.

The BROTHER's Gift.

The SISTER's Gift.

Nurse Truelove's NEW-YEAR's GIFT.

Death and Burial of COCK-ROBIN.

The ROYAL ALPHABET.

The HERMIT of the Forest, and the Wandering Infants.

Salem Mercury.

A new way to cure insanity.

A CURIOUS IDEA.

Knowledge is attained with the greatest difficulty; we have it not by intuition, but acquire it by many unsuccessful trials and long experience. One gives a hint, and the other improves it; but prejudice and ignorance too often stand in the way: "That cannot be," or "I cannot believe that," has crushed many an useful project. How incredible did the recovery of drowned persons appear at first! When the report reached England, that many abroad had been brought again to life, after laying under water some time, who gave it credit? But experience has since convinced us of its possibility.

Now, from the great success attending the recovery of drowned persons, I would offer a hint to the public, and leave it to be improved by them, respecting the recovery of those who are mad, and given up as incurable.

When madness breaks forth, the first care of the physician is to reduce and keep his patient low, in order to check the velocity and whirl of his thoughts; and if possible to procure sleep, by quieting the internal turbulency. If all his skill and efforts fail, such a person is as much lost to society as if he were dead. Now if such an one were plunged into water, and there kept until he was apparently dead, and was then recovered by the usual methods (and of which recovery we have now a moral certainty) I am apt to believe we should behold a perfect cure. There is, I own, something

shocking to nature in the experiment; but if the patient be already lost, and dead to society, why should we hesitate a moment to make the trial, when the probability of succeeding is so flattering?
Salem Gazette, July 12, 1791.
It would be interesting to see the punch-bowl out of which the members of Congress drank in 1811, on the day succeeding the marriage of Mr. and Mrs. Pearson.
At Washington, Hon. Joseph Pearson, Esq. (Federal Representative from N. Carolina), to Miss Eleanor Brent, daughter of Robt. Brent, Esq., Mayor of the city.— ☞ The greater part of the members, the next day, left the business of the nation to attend the punch drinking, so that the House adj'd at an early hour.
Dec. 13, 1811.
As the following lines have the indorsement of a Hartford paper, we venture to reproduce them:—
From the New-York Daily Advertiser, May 10.
DESCRIPTION of CONNECTICUT.
HERE fond remembrance stampt her much lov'd names,
Here boasts the soil its London and its Thames;
Throughout her shores commodious ports abound,
Clear flow the waters of the varying ground;
Cold nipping winds a lengthen'd winter bring,
Late rise the products of the tardy spring.
The broken soil a labouring race requires;
Each barren hill its generous crops admires,
Where nature meanly did her gifts impart,
Yet, smiling, owns how much she owes to art.
But keen as winds that guide the wintry reign,
All bow to lucre, all are bent on gain;
As chance decreed, their various lots are thrown;
Its house each acre, every mile its town;
With gilded spire the frequent church is seen,
Sacred to him that taught them to be keen;
Eternal squabblings grease the lawyer's paw,
All have their suits, and all have studied law;
With tongue that art and nature taught to speak,
Some rave in Latin, some dispute in Greek;
Proud of their books, in ancient lore they shine,
And one month's study makes a learn'd divine;
Fond to converse, with deep designing views,
They pump the travelling stranger of his news;
Fond of his wit, but fonder to be paid,
Each house a tavern, claims a tavern's trade;

While he that comes, as surely hears them praise
The hospitality of modern days.
Yet brave in arms, of enterprising soul,
They tempt old Neptune to the farthest pole;
In learning's walks explore the mazy way
(For genius here has shed his golden ray);
In war's bold arts thro' various contests try'd,
True to themselves, they took their country's side,
And, party feuds dismiss'd, join to agree
That scepter only just that left them free.
Connecticut Courant, July 14, 1790.

Errors of the press.

The following paragraphs will shew how completely the sense is altered by the omission of a single letter of the word in Italics.

"The conflict was dreadful, and the enemy was repulsed with considerable laughter."

"Robert Jones was yesterday brought before the sitting Magistrate, on a charge of having spoken reason at the Barleymow public-house."

"In consequence of the numerous accidents occasioned by skaiting on the Serpentine River, measures are taking to put a top to it."

"When Miss Leserve, late of Covent Garden Theatre, visited the 'Hecla,' she was politely drawn up the ship's side by means of a hair."

"At the Guildhall dinner, none of the poultry was eatable except the owls."

"A gentleman was yesterday brought up to answer a charge of having eaten a hackney-coachman for having demanded more than his fare; and another was accused of having stolen a small ox out of the Bath mail; the stolen property was found in his waistcoat pocket."
Salem Register, 1827.

A CURIOSITY.

"We have often heard of the Lord's Prayer being written in the compass of a shilling, but have lately seen a piece of paper of that dimension, which contains, in manuscript, the Lord's Prayer, the Creed, the Ten Commandments, Psalms 117, 120, 127, 131, 132, 134, and 150; 9th chapter of Proverbs, Prayer of St. Chrysostom, two Collects, Prayer for the Royal Family, Nobility, Clergy, andc., andc., the Blessing, and Junior, 1702, the name of the writer. This curiosity is in the possession of Mr. John Reeder, of Brighton, who being an auctioneer at a sale where it was lately sold, purchased it on very easy terms. It is not legible without a good glass."
Columbian Centinel, June 5, 1790. Eng. pap.

In an old Salem paper we find the following:

☞ We understand the number of deaths in this town the past year was 234, of which 15 died abroad.

This reminds us of the curious jumble made in the first edition of Morse's

"American Gazetteer," published in Boston in 1797. In the description of Albany, N.Y., it says: "This city and suburbs, by enumeration in 1797, contained 1,263 buildings, of which 863 were dwelling-houses and 6,021 inhabitants. Many of them are in the Gothic style with the gable end to the street, which custom the first settlers brought from Holland."

The earliest American writer of whom we have any information was Peter Bulkley, who was born in England in 1583 and died in 1659 in Massachusetts, and wrote Latin Poetry and Sermons. The earliest poetic volume written in this country was by Anne Bradstreet, of Boston, born 1612, died 1672.

Salem Observer, 1834.

The author of these lines must have been one of the old school.

[The following was paid for as an Advertisement.]

The folloing lines were Presented to A lat skull mistres in this town by 4 of her skolers the morning after her mareg

MAY all Joiy and happiness Vait
To attend your nuptal stat
you our instructer and the Guid
of our early youth beside
as you Quit the plas
wich you fild with euery Gras.
Our Grateful Thanks are sure your due.
Except them thearfor from us fue.
Whos shur to you that pras is due.
Must euery sorro euery Cear be yourn
Forbid it Heauin and let it turn
to peas and Joiys next to diuin
Rise Glorious euery futer Sun
and Bless your days with Joiys as this has dun
let sorrows sese and Joiys tak plas
to briten euery futer day with equil Gras
and wen your cald from hence above
may you inioy your souors Loue
wee ever shall regrat our los
and yet with you wee all reioyss

Essex Gazette, May 14, 1771.

Boston school-books in 1790.

The School Committee in Boston have ordered that the following Books be used in the Reading Schools of that town, viz.

The HOLY BIBLE;

WEBSTER's SPELLING-BOOK;

The Young Ladies' ACCIDENCE;

Webster's American SELECTION of Lessons in Reading and Speaking;

The CHILDREN'S FRIEND;

MORSE's GEOGRAPHY abridged; and

The NEWSPAPERS, occasionally.

Salem Gazette.

ANECDOTE.

When Oliver Cromwell first coined his money, an old cavalier looking upon one of the new pieces, read this inscription on one side, God with us; on the other side, The Commonwealth of England. I see, said he, God and the Commonwealth are on different sides.

Salem Mercury, June 26, 1787.

Two different ways of telling a story.

Anecdote. A CLERGYMAN, who in the Matrimonial Lottery had drawn much worse than a blank, and, without the patience of Socrates, had to encounter the turbulent spirit of Xantippe, was interrupted in the middle of a Curtain Lecture, by the arrival of a pair, requesting his assistance to introduce them to the blessed state of Wedlock. The poor Priest, actuated at the moment by his own feelings and particular experience, rather than a sense of canonical duty, opened the book, and began: "Man, that is born of a Woman, hath but a short time to live, and is full of trouble, andc., andc.," repeating the burial service. The astonished Bridegroom exclaimed, "Sir! Sir! you mistake, I came here to be married, not buried!" "Well (replied the Clergyman), if you insist on it, I am obliged to marry you—but believe me, my friend, you had better be buried."

Columbian Centinel, March 12, 1791.

Anecdote. It is doubtless recollected that Dean Swift, though a great favorite among the ladies, was (no doubt for good and substantial reasons) nevertheless a bachelor. His opinion of the married state seemed to be not very much exalted. On one occasion, he had been called upon to marry a couple, and after getting them properly arranged, commenced as follows: "Man, that is born of a woman, hath but a short time to live, and is full of misery," andc. "My dear sir," interrupted the bridegroom, "you are reading the burial service, instead of the matrimonial." "Never mind, friend," whispered the Dean, "you had better be buried than married."

Salem Observer, 1834.

AN OPPOSITION.

Dryden and Otway lived opposite to each other in Queen-street. Otway coming one night from the tavern, chalked upon Dryden's door, Here lives John Dryden, he is a wit. Dryden knew his hand writing, and next day chalked on Otway's door, Here lives Tom Otway, he is oppo-site.

Essex Register, 1802.

Specimens of old time newspaper poetry.

To a LADY who admired dancing.

MAY I presume in humble lays,

My dancing fair, thy steps to praise?
While this grand maxim I advance,
That all the world is but a dance,
That human-kind, both man and woman,
Do dance is evident and common.
David himself, that God-like king,
We know could dance, as well as sing.
Folks who at court would keep their ground,
Must dance the year attendance round.
All nature is one ball, we find:
The water dances to the wind;
The sea itself at night and noon
Rises and capers to the moon;
The moon around the earth does tread
A Cheshire round in buxom red;
The earth and planets round the sun
Dance, nor will their dance be done
'Till nature in one mass is blended;
Then we may say the ball is ended.
Salem Mercury, July 29, 1788.
THE FOUNT.

☞ THE following—from the pen of a fair correspondent—cannot be read without PLEASURE and IMPROVEMENT.
LINES for a SCREEN.
TO BE WRITTEN BENEATH THE FIGURE OF "MINERVA HOLDING A CROWN OF OLIVE."
AH! lovely Ladies—while with care
Ye guard from harm your FACES fair;
While spreads the airy PARASOL
To shield you from the beams of SOL;
And many a FAN and VEIL and BLIND
Protect from each intrusive wind:—
And whilst ye deign to intervene
Twixt you and fire, the humble SCREEN!—
Oh! strive alike to guard your hearts
From VICE, and all her wily arts.
Your parasol let VIRTUE prove,
To ward th' attacks of lawless love—
Prudence will prove a screen to thee,
And let thy VEIL be MODESTY.
Attend my words, ye Fair, for know,
This Crown shall grace the worthiest brow.
ORA.

Columbian Centinel, July 27, 1814.
From the Gazette of the U. States.
IMPROMPTU.
On seeing a young Lady darning Stockings.
ALONG the stocking's foot, with ease and grace
Your fingers, lovely Mira, when you move,
On them with eye admiring I will gaze,
And drink deep draughts of all resistless love.
Assume thy gloves, my most enchanting fair,
When next your stockings you begin to mend,
For though full white the hose, they yet appear
As saffron yellow, near thy lily hand.
As constant as your all obedient thread
Does thy bright needle's devious path pursue,
So does each thought of my poor brainless head
For ever dwell, divinest nymph, on you.
Oft as thy needles pierce the yielding hose,
So oft thy beauties pierce my yielding breast:
Oh then compassionate my deep felt woes,
And bid awhile the polish'd needle rest.
Or if one idle minute you disdain,
On me be exercis'd your mending art,
Yes, lovely maid, to ease of my pain,
Come, darn the hole that rankles in my heart.
Salem Gazette, August 26, 1800.
THE WHITE CLOVER.
BY A LADY OF NEW HAMPSHIRE.
THERE is a little perfum'd flower,
It well might grace the lovliest bower,
Yet poet never deign'd to sing
Of such a humble, rustic thing.
Nor is it strange, for it can show
Scarcely one tint of Iris' bow:
Nature, perchance, in careless hour,
With pencil dry, might paint the flower;
Yet instant blush'd, her fault to see,
So gave a double fragrancy;
Rich recompence for aught denied!
Who would not homely garb abide,
If gentlest soul were breathing there,
Blessings through all its little sphere?
Sweet flower! the lesson thou hast taught,
Shall check each proud, ambitious thought,

Teach me internal worth to prize,
Though found in lowliest, rudest guise.
Salem Gazette, June 27, 1815.
CASTALIAN FOUNT,
AMERICAN POETRY.
A FRAGMENT.
The following beautiful lines were written on the death of a young lady in
Pennsylvania, whose dissolution was occasioned by her mistaking a
poisonous mineral for the flower of sulphur, and swallowing a spoonfull:
THUS, o'er the tomb of what she held most dear,
The weeping muse no common sorrow pours;
No common anguish prompts the falling tear—
No common virtues those she now deplores.
Dear hapless girl, was there no saving power?
Where was your guardian angel—where your friend?
Could nought prevent the fatal destin'd hour?
Nor pitying Heaven would hear or succour lend.
Then, if nor Heaven would hear—nor friends could save,
Be still, my heart, nor breathe another sigh;
Drop the last tear upon her early grave,
And let it teach you—that the best must die.

☞ A few original favours from our poetick friends would be very
acceptable.
Massachusetts Centinel, March 28, 1789.
From the New York Daily Advertiser.
The Sailor Boy.
DARK flew the scud along the wave,
And echoing thunders rend the sky;
All hands aloft! to meet the storm,
At midnight was the boatswain's cry.
On deck flew every gallant tar,
But one—bereft of ev'ry joy;
Within a hammock's narrow bound,
Lay stretch'd this hapless SAILOR BOY.
Once, when the Boatswain pip'd all hands,
The first was he, of all the crew,
On deck to spring—to trim the sail—
To steer—to reef—to furl or clue.
Now fell disease had seiz'd a form
Which nature cast in finest mould;
The midwatch bell now smote his heart,
His last, his dying knell it toll'd.
"O God!" he cried, and gasp'd for breath,

"Ere yet my soul shall cleave the skies,
"Are there no parents—brethren—near,
"To close, in death, my weary eyes?
"All hands aloft to brave the storm,
"I hear the wintry tempest roar;"
He rais'd his head to view the scene,
And backward fell, to rise no more.
The morning sun in splendour rose.
The gale was hush'd and still'd the wave;
The Sea-boy, far from all his friends,
Was plung'd into a wat'ry grave.
But He, who guards the Sea-boy's head,
He, who can save or can destroy,
Snatch'd up to Heav'n the purest soul
That e'er adorn'd a SAILOR BOY.
Salem Gazette, Oct. 29, 1805.

EARLY RISING.

WIVES, awake! unveil your eyes;
Sluggards, no more yawning;
See the Delphick god arise,
Bright Apollo dawning.
Husbands, rouse at love's alarms,
Drowsy slumbers scorning;
Rovers, quit your favourite charms,
Up! behold, 'tis morning.
Virgins fair, have at your hearts;
Hymen's torch is flaming;
Cupid whets his pointed darts,
And look! the rogue is aiming.
Fair the bud of beauty blows,
Mellow sweets are palling;
Crown us with the virgin rose,
And so prevent its falling.
See the charms that nature yields;
Why sleep away your duty?
Arise! the fragrance of the fields
Is friendly to your beauty.
Lads, for shame! abed till now!
Forsake them, and be wiser;
There's health and pleasure, you'll allow,
In being an early riser.
Bound with ivy, bound with vines,
Youth serenely passes;

Bacchus round our temples twines,
And sparkles in our glasses.
No longer drown the mind in sleep;
But breathe the vernal air!
Our hours may thus improvement reap,
And who has any t' spare?
Salem Mercury, May 17, 1788.
From the New Monthly Magazine.
On seeing a Tomb adorned with Angels weeping.
Though sculptors, with mistaken art,
Place weeping Angels round the tomb;
Yet, when the good and great depart,
These shout to bear their conquerors home.
Glad they survey their labours o'er,
And hail them to their native skies;
Attend their passage to the shore,
And with their mounting spirits rise.
Britain may mourn her Patriot dead,
And pour her sorrows o'er his dust:
But streaming eyes, and drooping head,
Ill suit those guardians of the just.
Parents may shed a tender tear,
And friends indulge a parting groan;
If these in mimic form appear,
Such pious grief becomes the stone.
But if the wounded marble bear
Celestial forms to grace the urn,
Let triumph in their eyes appear,
Nor dare to make an angel mourn.
Salem Register, 1819.
Varieties.
Origin of the word Dun.—Dunny, in the provincial dialect of several countries, signifies deaf: to dun, then, perhaps may mean, to deafen with importunate demands. Some derive it from the word donnez, which signifies give; but the true original meaning of the word owes its birth to one Joe Dun, a famous bailiff of the town of Lincoln, so extremely active and so dexterous in his business, that it became a proverb, when a man refused to pay, "Why do you not dun him?" that is, Why do not you set Dun to arrest him?—Hence it became a cant-word, and is now as old as since the days of Henry VII. Dun was also the general name of hangman, before that of Jack-ketch.
And presently a halter got,
Made of the best strong hempen tear,

And e'er a cat could lick her ear,
Had tied it up with as much art,
As Dun himself could do for 's heart.
Cotton's Virgil Tra. Book iv.

It is curious to observe that Dun, who, as we said before, was finisher of the law in the reign of Henry VII., had a son, who became a bailiff—This bailiff having scraped some money together, made his son an attorney, who changed the name of Dun to Dunning—the rest of the genealogy are well known.
Massachusetts Gazette, Aug. 29, 1786.

Biographical Correctness.—As a specimen of the accurate way in which Biographical Dictionaries are made up, the Enquirer refers to Dr. Watkins' volume, in which he writes down that John Adams "died in 1803."—And yet for 23 years after this date, the old patriarch was living in health and happiness. A still more ludicrous blunder appeared a few years since in a French Biographical Dictionary, in which it was stated that the now venerable John Jay, who yet lives full of years and full of honors, was a Frenchman, who, after having framed the Constitution of the State of New-York, and witnessed the close of the American revolution, returned to France—became a member of the French Convention, and was finally brought to the guillotine!—N.Y. Com. Adv.
Essex Register, Sept. 18, 1826.

The works of John Paul Richter are almost unintelligible to any but Germans, and even to some of them. A worthy German, just before Richter's death, edited a complete edition of his works, in which one particular passage fairly puzzled him. Determined to have it explained at the source, he went to John Paul himself and asked him what was the meaning of the mysterious passage.—John Paul's reply was very German and characteristic: "My good friend," said he, "when I wrote that passage, God and I knew what it meant; it is possible that God knows it still; but as for me, I have totally forgotten."
Essex Register, Oct. 9, 1826.

Origin of "Foolscap" Paper. It is known that Charles I. of England, granted numerous monopolies for the support of his government. Among others was the privilege of manufacturing paper. The water mark of the finest sort was the royal arms of England. The consumption of this article was great at this time, and large fortunes were made by those who had purchased the exclusive right to vend it. This, among other monopolies, was set aside by the parliament that brought Charles to the scaffold, and by way of showing their contempt for the king, they ordered the royal arms to be taken from the paper, and a fool, with his cap and bells, to be substituted. It is now more than an hundred and seventy-five years since the fool's cap and bells were taken from the paper, but still, paper of the size which the Rump

Parliament ordered for the journals bears the name of the water mark then ordered as an indignity to Charles.

A new version of "Yankee Doodle," from the "Salem Gazette," July, 1811.

YANKEY SONG.

[The following song was composed a few years since by a gentleman then one of the officers of the Salem regiment, to be sung at the military celebration of the 4th of July. Its wit and pleasantry continues it a favorite with the Yankies, and it was again sung by the Military at Lynn Hotel, and by the Federalists at Washington Hall, on the late anniversary.]

I.

Yankey Doodle is the tune
Americans delight in;
'Twill do to whistle, sing, or play,
And just the thing for fighting.

CHORUS.

Yankey Doodle, Boys; Huzza!
Down outside—up the middle—
Yankey Doodle, fa, sol, la,
Trumpet, Drum, and Fiddle.

II.

Should Great Britain, Spain, or France
Wage war upon our shore, sir,
We'll lead them such a woundy dance,
They'll find their toes are sore, sir.

CHORUS.—Yankey Doodle, andc.

III.

Should a haughty foe expect
To give our boys a caning,
We guess they'll find our boys have larnt
A little bit of training.

CHORUS.—Yankey Doodle, andc.

IV.

I'll wager now a mug of flip,
And bring it on the table,
Put Yankey boys aboard a ship,
To beat them they are able.

CHORUS.—Yankey Doodle, andc.

V.

Then if they go to argufy.
I rather guess they'll find, too,
We've got a set of tonguey blades,
T'out talk 'em, if they're mind to.

CHORUS.—Yankey Doodle, andc.

VI.
America's a dandy place;
The people are all brothers;
And when one's got a pumpkin pye,
He shares it with the others.
CHORUS.—Yankey Doodle, andc.
VII.
We work, and sleep, and pray, in peace—
By industry we thrive, sir;
And if a drone won't do his part,
We'll scout him from the hive, sir.
CHORUS.—Yankey Doodle, andc.
VIII.
And then, on Independent Day,
(And who's a better right to?)
We eat and drink, and sing and play,
And have a dance at night, too.
CHORUS.—Yankey Doodle, andc.
IX.
Our girls are fair, our boys are tough,
Our old folks wise and healthy;
And when we've every thing we want,
We count that we are wealthy.
CHORUS.—Yankey Doodle, andc.
X.
We're happy, free, and well to do,
And cannot want for knowledge;
For, almost ev'ry mile or two,
You find a school or college.
CHORUS.—Yankey Doodle, andc.
XI.
The land we till is all our own;
Whate'er the price, we paid it;
Therefore we'll fight till all is blue,
Should any dare invade it.
CHORUS.—Yankey Doodle, andc.
XII.
Since we're so bless'd, let's eat and drink
With thankfulness and gladness:
Should we kick o'er our cup of joy,
It would be sartin madness.
CHORUS.
Yankey Doodle, Boys; Huzza!

46

Down outside, up the middle—
Yankey Doodle, fa, sol, la,
Trumpet, Drum, and Fiddle.
"Going snacks."
At the time of the plague in London, a noted body searcher lived whose name was Snacks. His business increased so fast that, finding he could not compass it, he offered to any person who should join him in his hardened practice half the profits; thus, those who joined him were said to go with Snacks. Hence going snacks, or dividing the spoil.
Salem Observer, 1823.
A Word omitted by Webster. In a history of the second parish of Beverly, published not long since, a vote passed in 1776, to take measures to collect the "behindments" of certain persons in the parish, is noticed. "Behindments" meant arrearages.
Salem Observer, 1837.
The following curious collection belonged to Mr. Samuel McIntire, the architect of the South Meeting-House in Salem, whose spire is acknowledged to be one of the best proportioned and handsomest in New England:
FOR SALE,
Sundry Articles belonging to the Estate of Samuel McIntire, deceased.— VIZ.
1 elegant BARREL ORGAN, 6 feet high, 10 barrels; 1 Wind Chest of an Organ;
ENCYCLOPEDIA BRITANNICA, complete;
Paladio's Architecture, best kind;
1 Ware's do.; 1 Paine's do.;
2 vols. French Architecture;
1 large Book Antient Statues, excellent;
Lock Hospital Collection of Music;
Handel's Messiah, in score;
Harmonia Sacra;
Magdalen Hymns; Massachusetts Compiler;
1 excellent toned SPINNET;
1 excellent VIOLIN and Case;
1 eight day CLOCK, Mahogany Case;
12 Prints of the Seasons;
1 book Drawings of Ships;
1 large Head of Washington;
Number of Busts of the Poets;
2 Figures of Hercules, 2 feet high;
1 Head of Franklin, and Pillar, for a Sign;
Composition Ornaments;

Number of Moulding Planes, and sundry other Articles. Apply to
ELIZABETH M'INTIRE, Adm'x.
or to SAMUEL F. M'INTIRE, Att'y.
N.B.—The Subscriber carries on CARVING as usual at the Shop of the deceased, in Summer-Street, where he will be glad to receive orders in that line. He returns thanks for past favors.
April 30 [1811]. SAMUEL F. M'INTIRE.

Many years ago there was published in Boston a small volume entitled "Eliza Wharton, the Coquette. By a Lady of Massachusetts." It consisted of a series of letters said to be founded on fact. A young woman died at the Bell Tavern in Danvers in 1788, whose gravestone a few years ago might be seen in the old Danvers (now Peabody) burial-ground. We copy from the "Salem Mercury" of July 29, 1788, the following account:—

Last Friday, a female stranger died at the Bell Tavern, in Danvers; and on Sunday her remains were decently interred. The circumstances relative to this woman are such as excite curiosity and interest our feelings. She was brought to the Bell in a chaise, from Watertown, as she said, by a young man whom she had engaged for that purpose. After she had alighted, and taken a trunk with her into the house, the chaise immediately drove off. She remained at this inn till her death, in expectation of the arrival of her husband, whom she expected to come for her, and appeared anxious at his delay. She was averse to being interrogated concerning herself or connexions; and kept much retired to her chamber, employed in needle-work, writing, andc. She said, however, that she came from Westfield, in Connecticut; that her parents lived in that State; that she had been married only a few months; and, that her husband's name was Thomas Walker;—but always carefully concealed her family name. Her linen was all marked E.W. About a fortnight before her death, she was brought to bed of a lifeless child. When those who attended her apprehended her fate, they asked her, whether she did not wish to see her friends: She answered, that she was very desirous of seeing them. It was proposed that she should send for them; to which she objected, hoping in a short time to be able to go to them. From what she said, and from other circumstances, it appeared probable to those who attended her, that she belonged to some country town in Connecticut: Her conversation, her writings and her manners, bespoke the advantage of a respectable family and good education. Her person was agreeable; her deportment, amiable and engaging; and, though in a state of anxiety and suspense, she preserved a cheerfulness, which seemed to be not the effect of insensibility, but of a firm and patient temper. She was supposed to be about 35 years old. Copies of letters, of her writing, dated at Hartford, Springfield, and other places, were left among her things.—This account is given by the family in which she resided; and it is hoped the publication of it will be a means of her friends' ascertaining her fate.

Elizabeth Whitman was the real name of the stranger, and the following was the inscription on the stone:—

"This humble stone, in Memory of Elizabeth Whitman, is inscribed by her weeping friends, to whom she endeared herself by uncommon tenderness and affection. Endowed with superior genius and acquirements, she was still more endeared by humility and benevolence. Let candour throw a veil over her frailities, for great was her charity to others.—She sustained the last painful scene far from every friend, and exhibited an example of calm resignation. Her departure was on the 25th of July, A.D. 1788, in the 37th year of her age, and the tears of strangers watered her grave."

Although we recollect seeing the stone some years ago, when the whole inscription could be read, we visited the spot in April, 1885, and found only a small portion left,—a triangular piece, perhaps a foot and a half high on one side, at the bottom of which we could only make out: "A.D. 1788, ... the tears of strangers watered her grave." For years, young persons of a romantic turn of mind have visited the grave and chipped off small pieces of the freestone for relics. This modern habit of chipping monumental stones for relics is inexcusable; for it is not done by ignorant or otherwise lawless persons, but too often by the educated, who carry their mawkish sentiment to such an extreme as to deface and sometimes, as in the present case, entirely to ruin a monument. It is in vain to urge that this was only a stranger's stone, and that there were none to care. It was all the more an outrage, if there were no friends to protect it. We are glad to learn that there were people in the town who did what they could to prevent this sacrilege.

The following account of this unfortunate lady we take from Hanson's "History of Danvers:"—

"Elizabeth Whitman came from a very respectable family in Connecticut, where her father was a clergyman. She was possessed of an ardent poetical temperament, an inordinate love of praise, and was gifted with the natural endowment of beauty and perfect grace, while she was accomplished with those refinements which education can bestow. She was lovely beyond words. But her natural amiabilities were warped and perverted by reading great numbers of romances, to the exclusion of almost all other reading. She formed her idea of men by the exaggerated standards she saw in the books to which she resorted; and thus when she looked around her she saw no one who realized her ideal. She subsequently became intimate with a lawyer, said to be the Honourable (?) Judge Pierpont Edwards."

We next hear of her in Danvers, "where the novelty of her situation," continues Hanson, "and her attractive beauty and manners during her short sojourn, caused the entire village and many from the neighboring towns to attend her funeral. A few weeks after her burial, an unknown hand erected the gravestone with its eloquent inscription." The stone is evidently

Connecticut sandstone or freestone. Mr. Hanson says of the volume "Eliza Wharton": "The catchpenny volume of letters which pretend to give her history has but the figments of the imagination of its authoress to recommend it."

Picture of the old Bell Tavern in Danvers. From the "Salem Gazette," January, 1781.

Danvers, Jan. 1781.

Just published,

And to be SOLD by

E. RUSSELL,

at his Printing-Office,

near the Bell-Tavern;

The Second Edition of

Russell's American ALMANACK,

For the Year of our Redemption, 1781.

Being First after Leap Year; and Fifth Year of Independency. Fitted for the Meridian of Boston, N. E. Lat. 42: 25 N. Wherein may be found all Things necessary for this Work.

To which is added, a Declaration of the Rights of the Inhabitants of the Commonwealth of Massachusetts, extracted from the Frame of Government; and a List of the Chief Officers of Government, which is thought necessary to be possessed by every Freeman in this Commonwealth.

Calculated by that curious and accurate Astronomer, BENJAMIN WEST, Esq; of Providence, State of Rhode-Island.

At the same Place may also be had, just published;

The Remarkable Captivity and Redemption of

ELIZABETH HANSON,

Wife of Mr. John Hanson of Knoxmarsh at Kecheachy, in Dover Township, who was taken Captive with her Children and Maid-Servant, by the Indians in New-England, in the Year 1724.

IN WHICH ARE INSERTED

Sundry remarkable Preservations, Providences, and Marks of Care and Kindness of Providence over her and her Children, worthy to be remembered.

The Substance of which was taken from her own Mouth, and now published for general Service.

The Third EDITION,

Also, an entertaining Narrative of the cruel and barbarous Treatment and extreme Sufferings of

Mr. JOHN DODGE,

During his Captivity of many Months among the British, at Detroit.

IN WHICH IS ALSO CONTAINED,

A particular Detail of the Sufferings of a Virginian, who died in their Hands.

Written by himself; and now published to satisfy the Curiosity of every one throughout the United States.

The Second EDITION.

*** All the above Books, with a Variety of other small Books, andc. will be sold to Shop keepers, Travelling-Traders, andc. at the very lowest Rate, if they purchase by the Hundred, Groce or Dozen.

In these sceptical and agnostic days it may sound a little strange, and perhaps to some seem quite absurd, that the authorities of Harvard in 1791 felt obliged publicly to deny that Gibbon's History was used as a text-book at the University. But with the exception perhaps of Tom Paine, no one in this country had then ventured to assail the literal interpretation of the Scriptures. Probably the masses of the people then believed that "Joshua commanded the sun and moon to stand still, and they obeyed him," that Jonah was swallowed by the whale, and that

"In Adam's fall,
We sinned all."

Of course there were exceptions. Therefore, although Gibbon might be an able writer, it was not safe for young men to study his works, simply because he had thrown doubt or derision on the Christian miracles. So when it was reported that a growing liberality of sentiment was being manifested at Cambridge, and that Gibbon's "Decline and Fall" was to be used, doubtless no little excitement was roused; and hence the notice. Before this time doubts concerning many cherished doctrines had been openly expressed in Boston, Cambridge, Salem, and other places; but Gibbon had rejected and attacked the whole Christian system as false, which was a very different matter.

For the CENTINEL.

Mr. Russell,

A WRITER in the Centinel of the last Saturday, under the signature of Christianus, says, "that an abridgment of Gibbon's history (if his information be true) is directed to make a part of the studies of the young gentlemen at our University." I now beg leave, through the channel of your paper, to acquaint that writer, as also the publick, that his information is not true. The system taught is Millot's Elements of General History, ancient and modern, and Gibbon's history was never thought of for the purpose.

JOSEPH WILLARD, President.

Cambridge, Nov. 14, 1791.

The Cholera.—It is worthy of remark that the word occurs in two passages of the Bible, both in Ecclesiasticus, and both places in connexion with directions and exhortations to a sober temperate mode of living, which is still recommended as the best preservative against this disorder.

Salem Observer, 1832.

The character of Boston ladies in 1788 is set forth in a letter in the "Herald of Freedom." The writer gives his observations on the error of committing children too much to the care of nurses; also makes reference to teaching the catechism, etc., showing the value of early religious training. There can be no doubt, we think, that the old methods were in some respects superior to the present, where in many cases young children are left to Sunday-school teachers, or, as is often the case, receive no religious instruction whatever, for fear, as we have often heard it stated, that they might imbibe some false doctrinal notions at an age when the deepest impressions are made.

For the HERALD of FREEDOM.

Letter IX.

DEAR PIERRE,

No moments glide away more agreeably than those that are employed in writing to a friend. Happy am I in having frequent opportunities of exhibiting my sentiments to you, and in return receiving yours, which palliates in some degree, the sorrow our separation occasions.——The glaring absurdities of the dress of the Boston ladies, occupied the greatest part of my two last letters. It is but just to say something of their more laudable qualities; amongst which, maternal affection deservedly claims precedence.—The barbarous customs of Europe, in this particular, have not as yet, and I hope never will be, practised here. Mothers in this country are so much attached to their tender offspring, as to forego all the pleasures of life (or rather what are so termed in Europe) in attending to their nurture, from which they derive the most superlative of all enjoyments, the heart-felt satisfaction of having done their duty to their God and country, in giving robust, healthy and virtuous citizens to the State. The effeminacy of exotic fashion has not at present extended its pernicious influence so far as to induce them to commit the rearing of their children to mercenary nurses, who are sometimes the very dregs of a people; and whose vicious habits of taking a drop of the good creature to drown sorrow, does not promise redundancy of health and vigour to those suckled by them—on the contrary, children thus unnaturally thrown from the arms of a parent into those of a nurse, are, almost without exception, weak and puny; of irrascible tempers and vicious inclinations.—Nor does the attention of the ladies expire with the infancy of their children—they still are unwearied in instructing them as they increase in years, and assiduously endeavour to inculcate principles of virtue into their young minds at a time when they are most liable to make a deep impression—to accomplish which, they never fail to teach them the catechism, Lord's prayer, andc. andc. all of which they oblige them to learn, because they are perfectly adapted to their comprehension, though many parts of the catechism are altogether incomprehensible to most adults.—Yet this is not strange to those who credit the scriptures; nor does it appear the least inconsistent—for there it says, "God hath chosen the foolish things of this world to confound the wise."—Therefore, the wonder that children should be able to understand that, which is the foundation of all polemical divinity, vanishes, when we try it by the touchstone of scripture, which is the criterion by which we ought to judge.—When they are thus instructed in the rudiments of virtue, they are seldom known to apostatize; so that for a native to become dissolute and abandoned, is very rare.—Indeed they have characters of this kind who emigrate from old countries; but they soon find employment for such gentry, by obliging them to labour for the publick good, and "work out their salvation by the sweat of their brow."—Thus the community is not only delivered from such pests, but experience beneficial effects from their confinement. Knavery, though rarely found in a native, is not entirely extirpated from the breasts of some among them.

Remarkable instances of longevity.

Longevity. Mafeus, who wrote the history of the Indies, which has always been a model of veracity as well as elegant composition, mentions a native of Bengal, named Numas de Cugna, who died 1566, at the age of 370. He was a man of great simplicity and quite illiterate; but of so extensive a memory, that he was a kind of living chronicle, relating distinctly and exactly what had happened within his knowledge in the compass of his life, together with all the circumstances attending it. He had four new sets of teeth; and the color of his hair and beard had been very frequently changed from black to grey, and from grey to black. He asserted that in the course of his life, he had 700 wives, some of whom had died, and the others he had put away. The first century of his life passed in idolatry, from which he was converted to Mahometanism, which he continued to profess to his death.—The account is also confirmed by another Portuguese author, Ferdinand Lopez Casteguedo, who was historiographer royal.

Salem Observer, Feb. 22, 1834.

LONDON, May 28.

Remarkable Instances of Longevity in Europe.

Thomas Parre, of Shropshire, died on the 16th of November, 1635, aged 152.

James Bowes, of Killinworth, in Shropshire, died the 15th of August, 1656, aged 152.

Anonymous, of Yorkshire, aged 140, and his son, aged 100, were both living, and attended to give evidence at York Assize, in 1664.

F. Sagar, of Lancashire, died in January, 1668, aged 112.

Henry Jenkins, of Yorkshire, died on the 8th of December, 1670, aged 169.

Robert Montgomery, of Yorkshire, was living in 1670, aged 126.

Countess of Desmond, Ireland, aged 140.

Mr. Ecleston, of Ireland, died 1691, aged 143.

Mr. Lawrence, of Scotland, living, aged 140.

Mary Gore, born at Collinworth, in Yorkshire, lived 100 years in Ireland, and died at Dublin in 1727, aged 125.

Mr. Ellis, of Surrey, died about 1748, aged 137.

Simon Sack, of Trionia, died on the 30th of May, 1761, aged 141.

Col. Thomas Winsloe, of Ireland, died on the 12th of August, 1766, aged 156.

Francis Consist, of Yorkshire, died in January, 1768, aged 150.

Francis Bons, of France, died on the 6th of February, 1769, aged 124.

Christopher Jacob Drakenberg, of Norway, a boatswain in the Danish navy, died on the 24th of June, 1770, aged 146.

Margaret Forster, of Cumberland, aged 136.

Gen. Oglethorpe died in August last, aged 103.

A goldsmith, of France, died in June, 1776, aged 140.

Mary Yates, of Shropshire, died in 1776, aged 128.

John Brookley, of Devonshire, living in 1777, aged 134.

Miss Ellis, daughter of Mr. Ellis, of Surrey, died in 1781, aged 104.

Mr. Froome, of Holms-Chapel, in Cheshire, died in May last, aged 125.

Mary M'Donald, county of Down, in Ireland, died on the 16th of June last, aged 118.

Mary Cameron, of Invernessshire, in Scotland, died in July last, aged 130.

Miss Ellis, of Richmond, in Surrey, living on the 16th of August last, aged 105.

Mr. Rowe, at Nutwell-House, in Scotland, died in August last, aged 106.

Donald McKeen, of Argyleshire, in Scotland, died in September last, aged 109.

John Button, of Liverpool, died on the 18th of November last, the oldest burgess of that borough upon record; he lived in six reigns, being born in the reign of James II.

Mr. Smith, a farmer, at Dolver, in Montgomeryshire, died in November last, aged 103: He was never known to drink any thing but buttermilk.

John Follart, woolcomber, at Norney, near the city of Exeter, living and in good health on the 30th of November last, aged 121; he works still at his business, and retains his faculties.

Massachusetts Gazette, Sept. 1, 1786.

PHILADELPHIA, August 19.

Instances of Longevity in America.

In South-America there was said, in the year 1785, to be a negro woman living, aged about 175; she remembered her first master, who died in 1615, and that he gave her away with some other property towards sounding a school.

Some years ago there was living in Virginia, a native of Ireland, who at the age of 109, was able to work at the taylor's trade without spectacles; and what renders this case more remarkable, he was naturally very intemperate, and would get drunk as often as he could get liquor.

In the year 1776, died one Mr. Payne, in Fairfax, Virginia, upwards of 100 years of age.

Died, November, 1782, in this city, Mr. Edward Drinker, almost 102, being born December 24, 1680, in Philadelphia.

In the year 1782, there was living, near this city (and perhaps may be still living) a healthy negro woman, able to walk several miles in a day, and wash clothes, who was then, as near as she could tell, about 103.——She remembers her being brought to this city before any houses were built here.

Died last summer, in New-York, Mrs. Slock, aged 108 years and one half.

Last winter died at Jones's creek, a branch of Pee Dee, in North-Carolina, Mr. Mathew Bayley, aged 136: he was baptised when 134 years old; had good eye sight, strength of body and mind until his death.

There was a woman living last winter, in Uxbridge, state of Massachusetts, of the name of Aldrich, and likely to live many years, who has 12 children, all living, and has lived till 25 of the fifth generation are born, the eldest of which is more than eleven years of age.

Died on Tuesday the 1st inst. at Hudson, in New-York, Mrs. Christina de Lametter, in the 94th year of her age. She died merely of old age, without any kind of disease or fever; but descended very slowly and patiently to the bottom of the hill of life. She was a woman, who, through life, has been remarkable for her silent resignation to the divine will. What renders the last part of her life remarkable, is, that she lived 39 days without any sustenance whatever, except about two spoonfuls of wine with water daily; the vital motions and functions being so near a cessation, that the solids needed no reparation; yet she retained all her senses to the last moment.

In the year 1774, died at Danvers, in Massachusetts, Mr. —— Nelson, aged 106 years.

Massachusetts Gazette, Sept. 1, 1786.

STOCKHOLM, Aug. 8.

A widow lately died near Landscrone, aged 118 years. She continued to get a livelihood by spinning till she was 116.

Salem Mercury, Nov. 25, 1786.

DINNER IN "OLD TIMES."

It was an old custom in New England to begin dinner with pudding instead of soup. Many persons of the last generation may remember, as the writer distinctly does, seeing old people who still adhered to this practice as late certainly as from 1850 to 1860. The writer was once at a dinner where all the family began with soup except the father, a gentleman of the old school, who had a piece cut from a fresh-baked plum-pudding. He remarked to the company that such had always been his practice; and so he excused himself for keeping to his own fashion of dining. The custom of eating pudding before meat is still very common in Yorkshire, England. The following extract from a Boston paper of 1819 shows that John Adams, in 1817, kept up the old style of dinner, which, as might perhaps be imagined, was not confined to the common people, so called.

In "old times" it was customary to say to children, "Those who eat the most pudding shall have the most meat."

Extract from the "Narrative of a Journey of 5000 miles through the Eastern and Western States of America," in 1817.—By Henry B. Fearon, an Englishman.

PRESIDENT ADAMS.

The ex-president is a handsome old gentleman of eighty-four; his lady is seventy-six: she has the reputation of superior talents, and great literary acquirements. I was not perfectly a stranger here, as a few days previous to this I had received the honor of an hospitable reception at their mansion. Upon the present occasion the minister (the day being Sunday) was of the dinner party. As a table of a "late king" may amuse some of you, take the following particulars:—first course, a pudding made of Indian corn, molasses and butter;—second, veal, bacon, neck of mutton, potatoes, cabbages, carrots, and Indian beans; Madeira wine, of which each drank two glasses. We sat down to dinner at one o'clock; at two, nearly all went a second time to church. For tea, we had pound cake, sweet bread and butter, and bread made of Indian corn and rye, similar to our brown home-made. Tea was brought from the kitchen, and handed round by a neat white servant girl.

The establishment of this political patriarch consists of a house two stories high, containing, I believe, eight rooms; of two men and three maid servants; three horses and a plain carriage. How great is the contrast between this individual, a man of knowledge and information—without pomp, parade, vitious and expensive establishments, as compared with the costly trappings, the depraved characters, and the profligate expenditure of —— House, and ——! What a lesson in this does America teach! There are now in this land no less than three Cincinnati!

Hogs in New York streets.

Yesterday forenoon, while in Broadway, we witnessed another instance of the impropriety of suffering Hogs to run at large in our streets. A highly respectable and most worthy young lady, was literally run down by a large Hog that was pursued by a dog. In her fall, her breast struck the curb stone, and she was considerably injured. After she had partially recovered, the gentleman at whose store she had made some purchases, kindly conveyed her to her father's house in a carriage. The reader may easily imagine the distressing effect produced on the mind of a fond parent, at the sight of a darling child, whose pale cheeks plainly indicated her situation. ☞ What would not the citizens of Boston say of their Police, if Hogs were permitted to run loose in the streets?

Columbian Centinel, Boston [1817].

English blunders about America in 1802.

From the (Newyork) Evening Post.

Specimens of the Ignorance and Blunders of English Geographers, Tourists, andc. andc. with respect to America.

THE Rev. R. Turner, who has published a book called Classical Geography, gives the following account of the cities of Philadelphia and Newyork. "Philadelphia, (says he) is the finest and best situated city in America, containing thirty thousand houses and one hundred and twenty thousand inhabitants, who are mostly quakers!!!"—"Newyork contains three thousand houses and twelve thousand inhabitants!"

Another book, intitled Guthrie's improved Geography, after setting forth in the preface that their (the Editors) relation of America, will be found both satisfactory and complete, as they have not only carefully examined the works of the celebrated Morse, but likewise applied to several other authentic sources, which have enabled them to give the best information in the most satisfactory manner, states that "the city of Newyork contains five thousand inhabitants, chiefly of Dutch extraction." Here is pretty strong evidence of the diligence of these London bookmakers, as to applying to the most authentic sources of information, as they profess to have done. An imposition of this kind in any American publication, would afford a fine opportunity for an English Reviewer to rail against our national honesty.

The very last edition of Guthrie's original work, describing the river Hudson, states that this river is navigable to Albany, which is "six hundred miles from Newyork."

An English Tourist, whose name is not just now recollected, has published a volume of his travels through the United States, in which he speaks particularly of the orderly manner in which Elections are conducted in the city of Newyork. "On the appointed day, says he, all the citizens take care to be at home at a certain hour, at which time the inspectors of the election go through the city with ballot boxes in their hands, and call at every door for votes, whereupon the citizens step to their doors and deposit their ballots in these same small boxes, which are straightway carried to the City Hall; the votes are there examined, and thus the election is determined in a few hours, without uproar or inconvenience!!!"

An English Editor of a work, called the German Museum, in his translation of some memoirs of Major André, records, that this unfortunate officer was taken and hanged "at the west point of America."

A London paper some time ago made mention of certain improvements which were taking place in Newyork, with a view to promote the health of the city, and observed that our corporation were erecting a range of permanent wharves on one side of the city, which were to extend from Corlear's Hook to the Battery along the Delaware River!

Some notice shall be taken hereafter of the misrepresentations and falsehoods of Laincourt, Weld, Bulow, and a number of others, relative to the United States.

An AMERICAN.

Worcester Spy.

SECRET LOVE.

From a very rare volume of old Poetry.

The fountaines smoake, and yet no flame they shewe;
Starres shine all night though undeserned by daye;
And trees do spring yet are not seen to growe;
And shadowes move although they seem to staye;
In winters woe is buried summers bliss,
And love loves most, when love most secret is.
The stillest streame descries the greatest deepe;
The clearest skye is subject to a shower;
Conceit's most sweete, when as it seems to sleepe;
And fairest dayes do in the morning lower:
The silent groves, sweete nymphes theye cannot misse,
For love loves most, when love most secret is.
The rarest jewels hidden virtue yield.
The sweete of traffique is a secret game;
The yeere once old doth show a barren field
And plants seeme dead, and yet they spring again.
Cupid is blind; the reason why, is this,
Love loveth most, when love most secret is.

Salem Register, 1827.

George the Fourth.—The attributes of this potentate, who was the most popular monarch England has had for many years, are thus severely described, by Thomas Jefferson in his correspondence of 1789.

"He has not a single element of mathematics, of natural and moral philosophy, or of any other science on earth, nor has the society he kept been such as to supply the void of education. It has been that of the lowest, the most illiterate and profligate persons of the kingdom without choice of rank or mind and with whom the subjects of conversation are only horses, drinking matches, bawdy houses, and in terms the most vulgar. The young nobility, who begin by associating with him, soon leave him disgusted with the insupportable profligacy of his society; and Mr. Fox, who has been supposed his favorite, and not over nice in the choice of his company, would never keep his company habitually.

"He has not a single idea of justice, morality, religion or of the rights of men, or any anxiety for the opinion of the world. He carries that

indifference to fame so far, that he would probably not be hurt were he to lose his throne, provided he could be assured of always having meat, drink, horses and women."
Essex Register, Aug. 26, 1830.
President Stiles of Yale College on the public revenue.
Extract from President STILES's Election Sermon.
But I pass on to another subject in which the welfare of a community is deeply concerned, I mean the publick revenues. National character and national faith depend on these. Every people, every large community is able to furnish a revenue adequate to the exigences of government. But this is a most difficult subject; and what the happiest method of raising it, is uncertain. One thing is certain, that however in most kingdoms and empires the people are taxed at the will of the prince, yet in America, the people tax themselves, and therefore cannot tax themselves beyond their abilities. But whether the power of taxing be in an absolute monarchy, a power independent of the people, or in a body elected by the people, one great error has, I apprehend, entered into the system of Revenue and Finance in almost all nations, viz. restricting the collection to money. Two or three millions can more easily be raised in produce, than one million in money. This collected and deposited in stores and magazines, would, by bills drawn upon these stores, answer all the expenditures of war and peace. In one country it has been tried with success for ages; I mean in China, the wisest empire the sun hath ever shined upon. And here, if I recollect aright, not a tenth of the Imperial revenues hath been collected in money. In rice, wheat and millet only are collected 40 millions of sacks, of one hundred and twenty pounds each, equal to 80 million bushels; in raw and wrought silk one million pounds. The rest is taken in salt, wines, cotton, and other fruits of labour and industry, at a certain ratio per cent. and deposited in stores over all the empire. The perishable commodities are immediately sold, and the Mandarins and army are paid by bills on these magazines. In no part of the world are the inhabitants less oppressed than there.
Massachusetts Gazette, Sept. 29, 1786.
Religiously Inclined.—A gentleman perceiving a fellow leaning against the front of St. Paul's church yesterday, who was unable to stand without some such support, asked him if he was going to join the church. 'No,' replied Bottlenose, 'not edzactly to jine, but I'm only lean—leanin'—that way.'
New Era [1837].
Meaning of the word.
Gentlemen. How the signification of words alter in the course of a century. There was a time when all persons in England, below the rank of an Esquire, were divided into Gentlemen, Yeomen and Rascals. The former word is now used to signify the individuals of the first order—those whom you would take by the hand in the street, and sup with of an evening. The

second term retains pretty nearly its original meaning. But to make an application of the latter appellative at this time, would operate as an invitation to be knocked down. 'Gentlemen,' is used in opposition among the old chronicles to 'simple man,' and neither in any very exalted sense. It is on record, that the French Princess, De La Roche Sur Yon, receiving a sharp reply from a Knight, to whom she gave the epithet of 'Gentilhomme,' was told by the King, to whom she complained, that she deserved all she got, for so offending, herself, in the first instance. The lower people in England were commonly 'the Rascality'—equivalent to the 'Canaille' of the French, or our own significant Rabble of the present day.

In what sense do they use the word 'Gentlemen' in Congress—Eh?—Charleston Gaz.

Salem Observer, April 3, 1820.

Professional Anecdote of Dr. Franklin.

WHEN he came to Philadelphia, in 1723, he was first employed by one Keimer, an eccentric genius, as a pressman, for he was then printing an elegy of his own composition, on the death of Aisquila Rose—and as he had but one small font of types, and used no copy, but composed the elegy in the press, he could not employ him in the composition. Keimer was a visionary, whose mind was frequently elevated above the little concerns of life, and consequently very subject to make mistakes, which he seldom took the pains to correct. Franklin had frequently reasoned with him upon the importance of accuracy in his profession, but in vain. His fertile head however soon furnished him with an opportunity to second his arguments by proof.—They soon after undertook an impression of a primer that had been lately published in New-England.—Franklin overlooked the piece; and when his master had set the following couplet—

When the last trumpet soundeth,
We shall not all die,
But we shall all be changed
In the twinkling of an eye,
He privately removed the letter c, and it was printed off—
When the last trumpet soundeth,
We shall not all die,
But we shall all be hanged
In the twinkling of an eye.

Herald of Freedom, June 23, 1790.

SURNAMES.

In the Cambridge Chronicle of Saturday, August 1, 1772, is an advertisement said to have been taken from the Canterbury Journal, which beggars the list of surnames lately enumerated:

"Mary Scaredevil, widow of the late William Scaredevil, of Maidstone, does, by the assistance of the Almighty, intend to carry on the business of

Whitesmith, and hopes for the favors and recommendations of the gentlemen and ladies whom the late William Scaredevil had the pleasure to serve, which will be gratefully acknowledged by their most humble servant, MARY SCAREDEVIL."

Salem Gazette, Nov., 1805.

Launching of the "Grand Turk."

Thursday last being a very pleasant day, great numbers of people assembled to see the launching of the large and beautiful ship from Mr. Derby's wharf. They were, however, disappointed in the pleasure they expected, by her stopping when she had run about half her length: and all the efforts which could be made were ineffectual in getting her off at that time: the next day, however, with the aid of proper apparatus, and the assistance of the people assembled, she was again put in motion, and gained the water.—The name of The Grand Turk is revived in this ship, heretofore borne by a ship belonging to Mr. Derby, remarkably successful as a privateer in the late war, and which was some time since sold in India.

The ingenious Mr. Enos Briggs, from the North River, was the master-builder of the new ship Grand Turk.

A CARD.

Mr. E.H. DERBY requests his fellow-townsmen and others, to accept his sincere thanks for their ready and unwearied exertions to enable him to complete the launching of his Ship. May 21.

Mr. Cushing,

The following lines were addressed to the Ship Grand Turk, while launching. They are at your service.

Your's, Z.

The swelling waves roll joyfully along,
To greet thee, welcome to the azure main;
The gaping multitude in anxious throng,
Their ardent—vacant—tumult—scarce restrain.
Slow o'er the lubrick ways—immense—you move,
High o'er the stern your flowing honours stand,
In distant climes, on unknown seas to prove
The matchless glory of your native land.
For thee—the lofty Cedar nods alone,
The sturdy Oak its honours lopp'd deplores,
The forest mourns its tallest beauties gone
To waft Columbian treasure—to the Indian shores.
Doom'd to resist the rage of warring waves,
Whilst rushing winds impel your foaming way:
The firm built sides their utmost fury brave.
The tempest mock—and in the whirlwind play.
Safe may you reach your distant—destin'd port,

Nor rocks—nor treach'rous sands—oppose your fame,
May gentle winds your swelling topsails court,
And thousands shout you welcome home again.
Salem Gazette, May 24, 1791.
The oldest person who had lived in Salem up to 1791.
On Friday last, the venerable Mr. John Symonds, of this town, entered the one hundredth year of his age. He is the only male person who has arrived at that great age, from the first settlement of the town by the English in 1629 to this day.
Irish Litany.
Dublin, May 11.
To the Printers of the Rights of Irishmen.
Gentlemen,
I am enabled by an invisible power to communicate to you, a Litany sanctioned by me, and to be adopted by the professors of the patriotic religion of Ireland; a Litany which breathes the spirit of that freedom which I professed when on earth, and has been here on eternal record; if its principle and doctrine tend to enlighten and emancipate your country, it will add (if possible) to that indescribable happiness enjoyed by him, whom, without vanity, I may now call the virtuous and patriotic
MIRABEAU.
Elysium, 5th Feb. 1792.
THE LITANY.
1st. Let there be a free, equal, and general representation of your people in Parliament.
And all the people shall say amen.
2d. Let there be a reform of your church, an abolition of tithes, and let each sect maintain its own pastor.
And all, andc.
3d. Let the people of my terrestrial country be an example to your people, and let their freedom be your freedom.
And all, andc.
4th. Let the fetters which the nobles of your land have forged, be broken asunder; and let those who earn, distribute the bread of Ireland.
And all, andc.
5th. Let each man freely worship God according to the dictates of his conscience.
And all, andc.
6th. Let christians be philosophers, and let philosophers be christians.
And all, andc.
7th. Let the rich few no longer be supported by taxes on the many and unrepresented poor.
And all, andc.

8th. Let all the sons of Hibernia be free—yea, even as free as the negroes[D] of Africa.

And all, andc.

9th. Let truth never be deemed a libel, and let the Liberty of your Press be extended.

And all, andc.

10th. Let the noble (tho enlisted) sons of Ireland never become the hired assassins of their countrymen.

And all, andc.

11th. Let the army which eats the bread of Ireland, be her guardian and protector, and not the base invader of her rights and liberties.

And all, andc.

12th. Let him who first proposed a mortgage on the revenues of Ireland, be accursed in the annals of your country.

And all, andc.

13th. Let yourselves no longer be the slaves of religion, or sect, or party, but the united sons of freedom and philosophy.

And all, andc.

14th. Let the majesty of your king reflect the majesty of your people.

And all, andc.

Mirabeau scripsit.

Salem Gazette, 1792.

[D] Vide Wilberforce on the emancipation of the slaves.

Boston School of Fashion in 1807.

Robert Smallpeace,

At his DRESSING ACADEMY, and SCHOOL of FASHION, in Milk street, opposite the South door of the Old South,

REMINDS the Sons and Daughters of Fashion and Beauty, that tho' they may possess every latent excellence, yet they require the improving hand of Art, like rough diamonds, to obtain the polish and brilliancy of the first water. What is elegance of form or contour of beauty without improvement? like "a light hid under a bushel," or whatever can be conceived to be most unlike:— And it is a lamentable fact, that

Full many a mind is rear'd with toil and care,

To waste its worth—by SLOV'NLINESS in HAIR.

The tailor, or milliner, may encase us with taste and elegance; the dancing master teach us the steps of ease and dignity; the musician instruct us in our throats and fingers; and the preceptor may inform our minds; and yet, with all these accomplishments, can we even be PASSABLE, if the highest accomplishment of all be neglected? and the HEAD be left to its own "disorder worse confounded," exhibiting a "paltry crown of mud and straw," placed upon an "edifice of ivory and gold!"—and further—

What though the EYE voluptuous roll,

The FORM possess each heavenly grace;
Say, can they ANY HEART control,
Draw FRIENDSHIP near—bid LOVE take place,
'Till SMALLPEACE touch them!—he whose trade is,
T' make Gods of Men—and Goddesses of Ladies!

☞ SMALLPEACE has elegant apartments for Ladies and Gentlemen; and will be found constantly at "the post of honour," and attendance, to wait upon them.

Oct. 17 [1807].

Columbian Centinel.

The novels of 1833; from the "Salem Observer," July 13.

The decidedly bad moral tendency of some of the most popular novels of the times is forcibly depicted in a magazine recently established in England, by two of the sons of William Cobbett, in the following language:—

"Would you seduce a wife? Falkland shall teach you to do it with gravity and dignity. Would you murder? Eugene Aram shall show you its necessity for the public advantage. Would you rob? Paul Clifford shall convince you of the injustice of security, and of the abominableness of the safety of a purse on a moonlight night.—Would you eat? Turn to Harry Bertram and Dandy Dinmont to the round of beef. Would you drink? Friar Tuck is the jolliest of companions. Would you dance, dress, and drawl? Pelham shall take you into tuition. Would you lie, fawn, and flatter? Andrew Wylie shall instruct you to crawl upward, without the slime betraying your path. Would you yawn, doze, sleep, or dream? Cloudesly shall do it for you, for the space of the first volume."

THOMAS MOORE.

Hostile feelings to the Americans having been imputed to the poet Moore in the first number of the (London) Westminster Review, the following paragraph appeared in the London Times of the 4th Feb., 1824.

"In the first number of the Westminster Review, just published, there is an article upon a late work of Mr. Moore's, in which the writer says, 'Mr. Moore has resided in America, and, we understand, speaks of the Americans with unbounded dislike and contempt.' In this assertion we can confidently state, the writer is entirely mistaken. Whatever opinions Mr. Moore may have hastily formed, when a very young man, with respect to the character and institutions of the Americans, we know that he has long since learned to correct them, and to feel towards that people all the admiration and respect which the noble example they set to the other nations of the world demands."

Boston Telegraph, 1824.

From the "Salem Gazette," Sept. 6, 1811.

Aiken's blood-letting Sermon
for sale by Cushing and Appleton.

From the "Boston Transcript," Dec., 1834.

Old times.—Mr. Thatcher stated, in his Lecture before the Boston Lyceum, that the Old Latin School in this City was commenced two hundred years ago, according to the records of the Town, which begin at the same year. For a long time it was the only school; and there was no writing school among us until November, 1684, (just 150 years since.) Master Cheever presided over the Latin 38 years, till he died at 93. He was the teacher of two of the Mathers, and the second Doctor said of him in an obituary essay, with his own peculiar felicity, that

——to vast age he grew,
Till Time's scythe waiting for him rusty grew.

Lovell was his second successor, and held on 92 years, till in 1776 he left the town a Loyalist. The old gentleman had a house furnished for him in School street, and a garden that reached nearly to Court street, which his best boys were allowed to till; and they had also the privilege as a reward of merit of sawing his wood and bottling his cider.—The Lecturer remarked that this was the first manual labor school he had heard of.

A quotation from Scripture.

"In the same day shall the Lord shave with a razor that is hired."

From the "Salem Observer," 1840.

Literary Curiosity. The following letter was written by a young gentleman to his "lady love," under the direction and eye of a rigid old father. The understanding, however, between the lovers, was, that she should read only every other line, beginning with the first. Love is full of expedients.

Madam,—

The great love I have hitherto expressed for you
is false, and I find that my indifference, toward you
increases daily; the more I see of you, the more
you appear in my eyes an object of contempt.—
I feel myself every way disposed and determined to
hate you. Believe me, I never had an intention to
offer you my hand. Our last conversation has
left a tedious insipidity, which has by no means
given me the most exalted idea of your character;
your temper would make me extremely unhappy,
and if we are united, I shall experience nothing but
the hatred of my parents, added to their everlasting dis-
pleasure in living with you. I have, indeed, a heart
to bestow, but I do not wish you to imagine it is
at your service; I could not give it to any one more
inconsistent and capricious than yourself, and less
capable to do honor to my choice and to my family.—
Yes, Madam, I trust you will be persuaded that

I speak sincerely; and you will do me a favor
to avoid me. I shall excuse your taking the trouble
to answer this. Your letters are always full of
impertinence, and you have not the least shadow of
wit or good sense. Adieu! Adieu! believe me, I am
so averse to you that it is impossible for me ever to be
your affectionate friend and ardent lover.

www.ingramcontent.com/pod-product-compliance
Lightning Source LLC
Chambersburg PA
CBHW071116280526
45787CB00003B/1065